The Gift of Being Uncomfortable

The Gift of Being Uncomfortable

WENDY ATTERBURY

The Gift of Being Uncomfortable

This book reflects the author's lived experiences. To honor the privacy of others whose paths intersect with these pages, certain names and identifying characteristics have been altered while preserving the truth of the events.

The Gift of Being Uncomfortable ©
Published by: Pan Enterprises
Copyright © 2025 by Wendy Atterbury

ISBN: 979-8-218-81773-2
ISBN (e-book) 979-8-218-85892-6

First printing 2025

Printed and bound in the United States of America.

1 3 5 7 9 10 8 6 4 2

We delight in the beauty of the butterfly, but rarely admit the change it has gone through to achieve that beauty.

—MAYA ANGELOU

Acknowledgments

To my children, who have been my greatest teachers.

To my husband who loves and supports me, but doesn't always understand the "Why."

A heartfelt thank-you to Joanne Moyle for her editing, patience, and guidance in supporting this first-time author through a challenging process.

And, as always, deep gratitude to Spirit for never allowing me to stray too far from a soul agreement and intention.

Contents

Preface

I have always wanted to write a book, a spiritual book to be exact. Ideas started popping up in my head during my twenties. I would always write them down in my journals. I even bought a typewriter to sit and "write my book."

I was moving along in my life, and I had never written "the book" until one day, four decades later, I thought, *Well, maybe now is the right time to write my book; I should take a writer's workshop or something like that.*

I was terrible at English and I really did not "see" myself as a writer; however, during many psychic readings, it had been brought up that I was going to do this.

I decided to attend a writers workshop in San Francisco for a weekend in 2013. It completely shattered my idea of writing "My Book." They spoke to us about social media and said we should have a large number of followers, write blogs, and basically become established as a known entity before we were ready to write a book. Well, I am none of those. During one of the speaker's talks (she was very well known and someone I admired greatly as a spiritual healer), she turned to us at one point and said something to the effect of, "If you are supposed to write a book, no matter what, and you listen, you will." That statement was the only positive thing that stuck with me that weekend.

After returning home, I was sitting one afternoon thinking about the workshop and feeling completely out of my depth. I thought, *Well, I don't have thousands of followers on Facebook or Instagram.* I felt like it was a wake-up call to finally let this idea go. I was sad, but at least I knew.

Later that same day, as I was taking a shower, I could feel my spirit guides gather around me (I seem to listen better standing with water pouring over my head). I could feel their deep love and benevolent energy.

"Well, dear one, what if you wrote your book, your story, and one person read it and it helped them, truly helped them? How would you feel about that?"

They were quiet, and I felt so humbled that I started to cry. I stood in that shower with tears streaming down my face. "Well," I said back, "that would be fine; it would be worth it."

"Well, then you have your answer . . ."

I contracted with a book developer, paid a large amount of money, and started. Chapter by chapter, I went along. When the final edit came back to me, it was hacked down to seventy-five pages and it was terrible. I had never done anything like this before, but I knew this was no "book development."

I was devastated. I had just read *Walking Home* by Sonia Choquette, a world-renowned intuitive guide and spiritual healer who had written a number of very well-known books.

I decided I would call her and set up a reading. I had never had a reading with her before and I didn't send any prior questions before our session. I knew that Spirit would tell me what I needed to hear.

Immediately after our opening prayer before our session, Sonia said, "Did you write a book?" I told her my sad tale.

"Wendy, this is your *soul's* purpose. You are firmly on your soul's path; you are meant to do this. Here, I will give you my editor's name and number; tell her I asked you to call her."

Wow, her editor had retired and wasn't taking on any more clients, but she gave me the name of another competent editor. I contacted the new editor, and we set up a consultation, and I would pay her as we went along.

I sent her my seventy-five pages, and she sent me a beautiful email back. During our first consultation, she said, "You have all these stories, but I don't know what the book is about."

What is the book about? Long story short, I couldn't figure out what the book was about, and I put it away until last year—ten years on.

I was at Miraval Spa in Tucson, Arizona, with friends. I felt compelled to book an appointment with Tina Powers, a medium who would occasionally offer sessions at Miraval. I had worked with psychics, healers, and such, but never with a medium.

"Your guides are here and want me to address this first. Have you written a book?" she asked.

Shit, I thought I was going to talk to dead people.

"It needs more added to it to round it out, but your guides are saying to dust it off." We talked further about the book, and she gave me the name of her editor, who was helping her with her new book.

"Wendy," Tina went on to say, seeing the look on my face, "she is the real deal."

The journey I have taken in writing this book is punctuated by the fact that, in truth, I just wasn't ready to embark on it until now. It took me six months after my session with Tina to take it out and dust it off. I contacted her editor, and we began.

It would be an understatement to say I was uncomfortable starting this book again. Why? Because it felt so personal, and parts of it were raw and painful to revisit. But I knew what the book encompassed: my stories, my lessons, and my growth.

I learned to appreciate the gift of being uncomfortable, and recognize the appropriate name for this book. This has made me realize that I can't hide from those feelings, especially if I am going to put this book out into the world.

If this book has found its way to you, I am grateful.

Prologue

Karma . . .

I have always viewed Karma as a form of "cosmic justice," a type of reckoning or reward for my actions in this life or in past lifetimes. I recently had the opportunity, while listening to a channel, to consider a more accurate evaluation of the word "Karma."

Karma, to me, felt like it had components of actions I no longer had control over, acts committed in other lifetimes that created retribution or reward in this lifetime. Additionally, if someone acted in a hurtful way or in a manner lacking integrity that justifiably made me angry or upset, then, at some point, when they might face unpleasant or even terrible consequences, I would say, "Oh, that is their Karma for doing such and such." It felt satisfying to see them confronting "retribution" for their bad behavior.

Honestly, I don't think I ever witnessed something amazing happening to someone and thought to myself, *Oh, that is their Karma at play!*

It's an ancient Sanskrit word that, in its original form, means "action." Actions are the language of physical reality. Karma refers to the actions you take to rebalance yourself if you have taken some actions that bring you out of balance. It is making the free will choice to then take the actions necessary to maintain balance in your life.

The minute I recognize the need to rebalance myself, then I have used Karma appropriately (response-ability). If I don't rebalance, then the imbalance—or lesson, as I like to call it—will repeat until I understand what actions I need to take that reflect the new insight I have gained.

Later in the book, I will share a poignant example of this, regarding part of a session I had with my teachers (through a channel) after I had a stillborn baby, which was devastating for me. The following communication is part of that session.

Spirit assured me, it was nothing that I had done. There was some unfinished Karma with the soul of the baby and I needed to endure.

Writing this preface, I asked in meditation for my teachers to explain to me why they used the word "Karma."

The answer: *Because, dear one, at the time, with your belief and understanding of the word "Karma," it was the only way we could disavow you of the belief you held in your pain and suffering that it was your handling of some difficult events leading up to the death of the baby inside your uterus that caused his passing, and that simply was not the truth. Had we not spoken the truth to you, there is a good chance you would not have been able to get pregnant again because of this belief—that it was your "bad Karma."*

I recalled what transpired in the rest of our session. It was suggested I look at how I truly felt about having another child. I chose to look deeply into my fears and reservations and honor them—not as bad, but as worthy of being accepted. Once I was able to be honest with myself and lean into it, through the excruciating pain and fear this action (Karma) caused, I slowly began to open up a place inside for another pregnancy.

Perhaps this book relates to the use of my own Karma: an "action of exploration"—reflecting my spiritual growth throughout life and illuminating my relationship with God and Creation and my own place in it.

I've learned that every misstep and unexpected moment is a conversation with something larger than myself, a gentle nudge (and, at times, not so gentle) from the Universe.

I don't have all the answers, and as you will see, my journey is messy and unpredictable. But in those imperfect moments—when I show up despite the fear and doubt—I can truly connect with God and experience the grace of this life.

This is my honest, imperfect dance with the Divine.

Introduction

I was sitting at my desk in my home office, working on the concept for this book, when my husband, Harry, did something that made me so furious I screamed at him. "Jesus Christ, Harry! What in fucking God's name are you doing? Goddammit, Jesus, Mary, and Joseph—what the hell?"

Words tore from the depths of my soul with a force that stunned me into a silence of sudden awareness, as if, for the first time in my life, I realized that in a fit of anger I used the names of God, Jesus, Mary, and Joseph in the same way I would say, for example, "Fuck you!"

I thought my husband had accidentally deleted the music from my iTunes library, and yes, I was seriously pissed off. However, I apologized to him and considered the very purpose for which I was writing this book: to share my story, my experiences, strength, and hope. Here I am, standing at the threshold of the book, gazing directly into its soul, my soul—the essence of my being—which begins with . . . God. So why, in a fit of anger, was I cursing at God, Jesus, Mary, and Joseph? I suddenly wondered if Buddhists curse at Buddha.

"Oh my God, what a setup!" I said to myself, hands on the computer keys, sitting in stunned silence.

When Spirit truly wants to capture my attention, it sets me up. Usually, though not always, I can recognize it due to its excessive drama; I can sense the energy shift and feel an immediate pang of ego.

It's always done with love in a straightforward manner. Today was no different. I could start this book from my childhood and continue on, but I really have to begin with God because God is the foundation of my existence as a soul energy source. Raised in the Christian faith, I was introduced to Jesus, Mary, and Joseph. But why was I cursing at them? Why do I still curse at them?

Do I blame them on deep, conscious levels? Am I holding them accountable for everything that goes wrong in my life and in this world? It's interesting how I might say, "Oh, for God's sake, what are you doing?" or "Dear God in heaven, I hope that isn't true," or "Jesus Christ, what the hell?" I could keep going . . .

It certainly seems like I'm blaming them. Words carry weight; I now question the true power of their intent. Should I hold God responsible for all the wrongs in my life? My logic mind says, "No, of course not; don't be ridiculous." Yet here I was, sitting stunned at my visceral reaction to something I thought my husband did. For the first time in my adult life I am experiencing something so blatantly obvious, which had *never* occurred to me before.

CHAPTER I

In the Beginning

"All the world's a stage and all the men and women merely players; they have their exits and their entrances."

—WILLIAM SHAKESPEARE, *AS YOU LIKE IT*

I began life enveloped by love and high expectations. I completed our little family of four, along with my older brother, mother, and father. We all held deep within our psyche, as a family, individual expectations of what our lives would be like.

In my early years, my expectations intertwined with those of my parents and my brother. I came to look forward to our meals, enjoyed together with classical music playing softly in the background on my father's Hi-Fi, occasionally dancing the polka in the living room after dinner. There were trips to our local drugstore soda fountain for ice cream in the summer and vacations along the rocky coast of New England to visit my grandparents and spend time with my cousins. I cherished those trips to the sea. Of course, these joyful moments were also mixed with the occasional spanking and time-out. My mother was a stay-at-home mom, while my father commuted daily to the city by train. My life closely resembled the family shows being aired on local TV during the 1950s.

By way of my birth, I was taken to the local Episcopalian church to learn about Jesus, God, Mary, Joseph, and the Bible. It was all straightforward enough to me at that time. God was the Father, the all-knowing being who ruled over everything; Jesus was his only Son whom he sent to Earth to help all of us sinners and teach us about God. Mary was his mother, and Joseph was his earthly father. (I did not understand the concept of the Immaculate Conception as I was too young.) Jesus wandered around the countryside with little or no possessions, preaching to his followers about God, love, and true riches. It didn't seem to me, looking at the pictures in my Bible at the time, that Jesus liked churches much. I liked that about him because I would much rather have been outside playing than sitting in Sunday school. I also enjoyed hearing about the miracles he performed. He was so great that he scared the leaders, and they wanted to kill him because his followers called him the "King" of the Jews. Then, one of his closest followers betrayed Jesus, so he was arrested, nailed to a cross, and died to take away all our sins. (I was five, and already I was a sinner who needed to have my sins removed; I remember that confused me.) But then he rose again on the third day, which made me feel happy because then I knew he was magical and probably still alive to take care of me and everyone I loved.

Interestingly, the one strong reaction I remember from my indoctrination was when a Sunday school teacher emphatically told me one Sunday morning that anyone who did not embrace Jesus Christ as their savior would go to hell.

That's not true, I thought to my younger self. *Jesus would never do that.* It was a strong, visceral feeling in my solar plexus, and I was very put off by my Sunday school teacher. My dad never went to church or spoke of Jesus or God, as far as I can remember, but I "knew" my daddy was not going to hell.

In the setting of my little Sunday school class, I developed perhaps my deepest and most profound expectations. That God and Jesus loved me completely, even though I was "a sinner." They would always take care of me and my family, ensuring I remained safe and happy as long as I believed.

As an adult, I naturally think, *Well, that was unrealistic.* And yes, it was. At no point was any other idea mentioned or encouraged. My belief in God and Jesus, and that I was a sinner but Jesus had removed all my sins, had no relation to how the adults in my life behaved around me.

As a child, I would have episodes of what was termed then as ESP, or extra sensory perception.

I would awaken at night and see beaded energy fields circling my head; it always comforted me when I lay awake. I would turn over onto my stomach, with my face in my pillow, and see white light in the area of my third eye. I didn't understand any of it, but I was in my young body, connecting with other realms that felt familiar and comforting. Of course, I never mentioned this to any adults; it never occurred to me to do so. I remember having a family dinner at my grandparents' house in Padanaram, Massachusetts. During dinner, a lid from one of my grandmother's silver pitchers on the sideboard of the dining room flew off with a bit of a racket, to which I immediately responded, "Oh, that was Casper" (the friendly ghost). Even though children weren't allowed to speak at the table unless addressed, all the adults laughed and thought it was cute. I, however, wasn't joking, as I had encountered earthbound spirits in a friendly way in the house. As I grew older, I learned not to mention what I would now characterize as my gifts because it was deemed unacceptable.

It wasn't just that I had an odd vision now and then, but that I knew things; I felt things about the adults around me—things that came from realms beyond the physical. One summer, while vacationing in Padanaram, I was sitting with my father, mother, and brother outside my grandparents' house. My father had just returned from the train station, where he was picking up my Uncle Sam, his brother. Uncle Sam looked very different from the other brothers; he wasn't particularly handsome, and he was high-strung and fidgety. I could sense just how uncomfortable he felt around his family. He never married and struggled to hold down a job. His two older brothers had Ivy League educations and were doing well professionally (though not so much personally). My mother told me many years later that she always suspected he might have been gay. Uncle Sam had a good heart; I loved him, and it shattered me to see how he was treated and judged by the adults sitting on that lawn. He would squirm and chatter, trying to seem normal. To me, it felt like he was drowning, desperately trying to keep his head above water while the rest of his family stood by and watched. It made me sad. All I could do was watch; I was a six-year-old child—what did I know? Uncle Sam died in his fifties of cancer. I learned that while serving in WWII, the carrier he was on was hit by a Japanese kamikaze pilot, although he survived when many around him did not. He never recovered from the war; his nerves were completely shot, which added to his excessive drinking. Now, of course, the medical community knows a lot about PTSD. My little six-year-old self understood he was under incredible stress. I felt he wasn't being taken care of by his parents and brothers.

By the time I turned seventeen, all the carefully curated expectations I had about my life and the world around me were completely shattered. When I was eight, my father began having an affair with a woman he met in a coffee shop near his office. He left my mother when I was nine, and the ensuing divorce was ugly. My mother fell apart, started drinking heavily, and repeatedly slept with married men in our home. She would fly into uncontrollable rages at the slightest provocation.

My mother completely unraveled into a pattern of self-destructive behavior. She chose rage and alcohol as her coping mechanisms. In those days, it took time to get these matters through the courts for financial support. In the meantime, my mother, who had gone to business school, had training on a typewriter. Fortunately, one of her friends' fathers ran a school, and he offered her a secretarial position there, where she worked for over thirty years. My mother was a beautiful woman, well-read and intelligent. She loved theater and performed in local plays. In fact, she was a dramatic and theatrical person, which probably contributed to her highly dramatic screaming fits after my father's departure.

My father was a tall, very handsome man, and he was well-educated despite having severe dyslexia. The eldest of four boys, his parents had high expectations for him. He was incarnated into a very wealthy, strict New England family, which sadly lost a great deal of its fortune after the stock market crash in 1929. My father's god became money; all he ever wanted was to be a millionaire. He never completed university as World War II came around, and he enlisted in the Air Force. He was highly decorated for his service, but like all who serve, there was a price to pay. Even though he survived the war, he never spoke about it until he was much older.

In our neighborhood in the early 1960s, there were no divorces, and I did not have any friends whose families were experiencing divorce. Our home fell into ruin emotionally, physically, and financially. I used to help my brother with his paper route so we could use the money for food.

Before my father left, I would sometimes get in trouble at school for laughing; I was quite the giggler, which seemed to cause some consternation among my teachers. After my father left, I became very quiet and kept to myself. I remember in elementary school, my mother never allowed me to wash my hair, and she wouldn't wash it either—maybe once a month. Because of this, I always felt very dirty and unkempt.

I had been a happy-go-lucky girl, attending elementary school within walking distance of my house and living in a charming suburban neighborhood. Mom, Dad, my brother, and I were living the dream. Then, in third grade, everything fell into sorrow and chaos as my parents navigated a divorce. Where was the promise that God and Jesus would care for me if I believed? Now I felt very alone. I must have done something wrong; this was not how it was supposed to be.

As I entered high school, I was able to manage my hygiene, but I struggled with low self-esteem and feelings of worthlessness. I fell in love with my first boyfriend when I was in tenth grade, but he broke my heart.

Of course, there was also the world stage. By the time I reached my seventeenth year, war, famine, devastating pollution, and injustices were rampant, causing me immense anguish. I felt hopeless.

But most of all, I was really, really angry with God and Jesus. I expected better of them, and they were letting me down, as well as all of humanity. I did reach out to the religious community, attending more progressive Christian services and listening to priests and reverends, but I never saw anything in their eyes or words that I felt truly explained what was going on.

I woke one Saturday morning and decided I needed to go to the source, to speak with God and Jesus. Near my apartment was an area—a rolling green hill surrounded by thick woods at the rear of an unoccupied old estate built in the early twentieth century. The estate was one of the many large summer homes of the wealthy.

I referred to my spot as simply "the Hill." Growing on the crest of this gentle hill was a lone tree, surrounded on three sides by forest and sporting soft-tufted grass around its base. When I arrived, I sat down, taking extra care to get comfortable. I hadn't remembered to bring my journal, but it didn't matter. What I really wanted to do was "talk" to God and Jesus. I was filled with anger and frustration.

From my young perspective, since Jesus's ascension, we Christians had done nothing but create murder, mayhem, divisiveness, ethnic cleansing, and condemnation of all souls on the planet who did not embrace him as their savior—all in Christ's name. So, I sat down, in full possession of my anger, overwhelmed with a feeling of helplessness, and asked Jesus, "*What is going on here?!*"

I thought that if Jesus was truly vast and great, surely he could take a moment from his busy day to explain it to me! I sat under the tree for a while, with many fleeting thoughts passing through my mind, such as, *If Jesus appeared to me in human form right now, I would probably faint right away, but I'm willing to take that chance.*

Within minutes, a wave of sleepiness washed over me, prompting me to curl up into a little ball on the soft grass beneath my tree, with my spoken demand still nestled in my heart.

Then, I was abruptly awakened by a loud voice in my head saying, "Run back to your apartment building *now*!!!" Dazed and confused, I obeyed and found my good friend Alex coming down the steps of my building after just knocking on my door. He had stopped by to see if I wanted to take a ride on his new motorcycle. For a brief moment, all I could do was stare at him, speechless; it didn't make any sense to me at all. Why had I been told to run home just in time to catch Alex, right at the last moment for a motorcycle ride? Was this how they chose to answer my burning question? With a mundane, everyday event? *They must not have heard me*, I thought. But I went for my motorcycle ride, and we had a splendid afternoon.

Events in my life have created a seismic shift in my destiny. Unbeknownst to me at the time, I had sent out a powerful request to God and Jesus.

"What is going on here?!" was the question I asked. At the time, I didn't understand how that could possibly relate to listening to instructions to run home and then bumping into Alex as he exited my building. But it didn't matter; it wasn't the right time, and I wasn't ready to hear the answer.

As my time went on, the question I posed to God and Jesus that day never left the deep recesses of my heart. Alive and well, it presented itself in different forms—intuition, curiosity, and, on more than one occasion, slamming into the proverbial wall. Powerful moments of grace and insight were always there, pulling at me: "Look deeper, keep asking questions," seemingly out of my reach at times, but I could feel it (my guides made sure of that!). "Participate in your life and see what unfolds."

Throughout my life, I have experienced moments of grace, peace, and serenity, but they seem to have a very limited shelf life. I have always felt that something was missing—something I couldn't put my finger on. Deep in my heart, I knew there would come a time for a profound personal reckoning—not because I needed redemption or had strayed from Christianity and needed to be "born again." No, for me, this reckoning would not occur through religion or by reading the Bible or any type of scripture, for that matter. The kind of reckoning I sensed would transcend religion and lead me to the core of my being. *Who am I?* That was how I would mend my relationship with God and Jesus. Perhaps by understanding who *I am*, I would come to understand God and Jesus.

I explored past life regressions, worked with channels, healers, ministers, gurus, psychics, life coaches, trainers, doctors of Chinese medicine, holistic doctors, Al-Anon, a wide range of books, and my own spirit teachers.

No words could have been spoken that day to me on the Hill. Instead, I was awakened and sent running headlong into a large part of my destiny. With my questions firmly set in my heart, I stepped back onto my life's path to search for and live the answers I so desperately longed for.

My prayers and questions have *all* been heard and answered —never as I expected, but in more profound ways than I could ever imagine. By understanding who I am, I would better understand God and Jesus.

Reflecting on the moment when I found myself cursing Jesus, Mary, and Joseph in a fit of rage, I realize it was a direct setup from Spirit for the beginning of my story. It was only through writing my narrative that I recognized my expectations; the promise of my lifelong indoctrination into Christianity turned out to be a profound disappointment to me. In third grade, I was accepted into our choir, and I truly cherished standing by the altar singing hymns during the holidays; it felt like a peaceful sanctuary as my parents went through their divorce. My mother began singing in the adult choir and started a relationship with someone I recognized, as he would visit our home. I felt so embarrassed and ashamed, especially since his children sang alongside me in the choir, which caused me to stop attending and withdraw into a place of sadness and shame as our once-happy family imploded.

My anger and frustration went way beyond this lifetime, however.

While working on this book, I drifted into a past life memory one day while resting. I recalled being alive when Jesus was alive. I was one of his devoted followers, female and very close to him. I remembered loving him deeply and feeling a profound attachment, much like the bond I have with my children. When they suffer, I suffer; when they are happy and fulfilled, all is right in my world. I feel powerless to do otherwise. My experiences in this lifetime led me to Jerusalem when Jesus decided to enter the city, even though he knew he was going to be betrayed, arrested, and executed. I pleaded with him; I was furious at his choice. He was doing this intentionally, but why?

I watched him die on the cross with nails driven into him; I was utterly devastated . . . shattered. Why did he cut his life short? He had so much more to teach! I didn't get it at all.

When Jesus rose from the dead and his body was no longer where they had placed him, I even saw him in his ethereal form. It did nothing to alleviate my devastation. I wanted to hug him, look into his eyes, sit with him, and banter about mundane things. I was experiencing deep emotional pain and loss.

As I drifted back from this past life experience, I was deeply shaken. I lay still for a long time as tears streamed down my face. The reasons that Jesus lived and died in that manner began to dawn on me; a powerful understanding slowly emerged from the depths of my soul.

"I'm so sorry," I said into the stillness of the day. "I didn't know. I didn't understand."

I recognize that there are numerous religious interpretations of Jesus's death, but this is my personal experience and understanding as I awakened that day.

As I lay there crying and apologizing, I felt such a loving, peaceful presence. I was on my way to healing a deep past-life trauma that has informed many lifetimes. Imagine, in 2024, and years later, I still had this unconscious, habitual tendency to cuss at Jesus.

Reflecting on my time at "the Hill," when I was genuinely fed up with Jesus and God, I now grasp my answer a bit better. As puzzled as I felt when I was awakened and told to "run" back to my apartment—only to come across Alex, whom I nearly missed—my life lessons and spiritual growth were set to evolve through the "doing" of life.

Life is a living thing, an energy that is constantly in motion. Sometimes, it gets messy, complicated, and painful, but then . . . the grace, the magic . . . and the love.

All of it.

CHAPTER 2

Peace Is Within

When the student is ready, the teacher will appear.

"Is that the type of clothes you're wearing these days?" my brother asked me with a look of shock on his face. He was referring to my buckskin jacket, T-shirt, bell-bottom blue jeans, and Indian moccasins.

"Uh . . . yeah, pretty much," I answered.

In 1968, the hippie movement had made its way into the suburbs of Philadelphia. My newfound exploration of smoking marijuana and taking LSD began to propel me into a shift in consciousness, allowing me to experience the ordinary around me—especially nature, people, and my own thoughts—in exhilarating new ways. I embraced the hippie ethos; it felt comfortable and authentic, soon becoming my zeitgeist. Clothing made from natural fibers, organically grown food, freedom from social systems, an end to wars, and living close to the land in communes—all contributed to the hippies' mission of creating peace on the planet. Where did God and Jesus go? It didn't matter to me because the hippies had figured it out. This movement resonated deeply with my soul. However, the bright flash began to fade quickly as my focus shifted from using drugs to expand my consciousness to using them for self-medication. The vagaries of my past started to reemerge with a vengeance.

My psyche and my grades were both suffering significantly, so, after my second semester, I left my local junior college in Pennsylvania and flew out to the West Coast, where my brother had settled after completing his service in the Navy. I had graduated high school in the spring of 1969, feeling deeply grateful—at least by my standards at the time—that I was finally unfettered by the social pressures of high school cliques, popularity, athletic prowess, and conforming to standards of physical appearance. I was free to pursue the new path ahead being forged by the "hippie" movement.

My brother and I stood at the airport for a moment, sizing each other up, and then hugged. As we approached his car, a brand-new Datsun 240Z that he had carefully saved up to purchase, he said, "I'm only the third person in California to get one so far!"

"Oh. That is sooo materialistic."

My brother glared at me, and I instantly regretted my words as I felt them wound him. It was easy to eschew material things, especially when I couldn't afford them, but I knew how hard my brother worked. Suddenly, my judgmental words were being mirrored back to me.

While riding from the airport and during the following days, we talked a lot about the Vietnam War and our very different views on life. He was, after all, six years older than I. He under-stood that I had serious misgivings about war in general.

In turn, I realized that he believed serving our country, as our father had, was the right thing to do for a number of rea-sons. He didn't speak about his personal experiences or the pain of losing friends in combat. He didn't describe what it felt like to fire a weapon at someone who was trying to kill him at the same time. Maybe he wasn't ready to share those experiences with his family. However, he did share with me that when he returned home to the United States after his final tour, people actually spat on him in the airport. As he relayed this to me, I felt horrified and ashamed, and my involvement in the anti-war movement suddenly took on a new personal significance. Spit-ting on a soldier was an act of cowards; in the name of peace, they were spewing anger and hatred toward another human.

Although my brother never spoke about the deep trauma he experienced in the war (maybe a little with my father, who served in WWll), I realized that he went to chapel and grew in his faith and service to the Lord and Jesus. That connection and practice offered to him in the service were very sacred to him, and he and his wife practice it today. I watched it help him heal over the years.

I prayed every day for his safety. Back in those days at public school, we would have morning prayers, and I always prayed with all my heart for my brother to come home safely from the war.

One Saturday when I was fifteen, I was supposed to spend the day with my father and stepmother, as part of my parents' divorce agreement. When I arrived at his apartment, I noticed that he was deeply upset and agitated. He paced around the room and then set the morning paper on the table. On the front page of the paper was a picture of the USS *Forrestal* ablaze.

"Your brother is on that ship," he said to me as I sat there reading the article. (My brother flew on sea air rescue missions with the helicopter squadron.) I quickly realized how grave and devastating the situation was, and, of course, my father was unable to determine anything regarding my brother.

I calmly looked up from the paper and into my father's eyes and said, "He's fine; I would *know* if he were injured or dead."

Although my stepmother mocked and chided me about how serious it was, I *knew* he was fine. Indeed, he was fine as they were returning to the carrier from a mission when they came across the fire.

When I was eighteen, I had already participated in numerous protests. As demonstrators, we would smoke pot; consume psychedelic drugs; chant and drum alongside figures like Allen Ginsberg; prepare to attend peace marches in Washington, DC; and learn to volunteer in medical tents. It was exhilarating to be even a small part of that monumental shift in consciousness, a movement aimed at finally bringing peace to our planet and addressing the world's problems.

In Ram Dass's book *Polishing the Mirror*, which I read years later, that time was described beautifully in the foreword by Rameshwar Das.

The Gift of Being Uncomfortable

The year Ram Dass's first book, Be Here Now, *was published, 1971, the Vietnam War was provoking a backlash of protests. Ebullient waves from psychedelic drugs, acid rock, newfound sexual freedom, feminism, environmentalism, and back-to-the-land hippie communes were creating tectonic shifts in the existential landscape. The psychedelic expansion of consciousness began crossbreeding with Buddhism, Hinduism, and new age spirituality to offer glimmers of internal liberation.*

On one particularly hot, steamy summer day, I attended a peace rally in Washington, volunteering in a medical tent. While Jane Fonda spoke, things were slow in the medical tent, so I sat and watched the crowd while listening to her voice. It suddenly dawned on me that only about a third of the people at the rally were actually paying attention to her message. The rest were partying, running around half-naked, and jumping into fountains. They behaved as if they couldn't care less about peace —or the war.

Until that moment, I had thought with complete certainty that we were truly going to bring about peace. We were going to stop killing one another, polluting the planet, and being so materialistic. I genuinely believed this. Of course, I was terrified that my brother would be killed in Vietnam, so I fervently wished to see an end to the Vietnam War!

During the rally, as I watched the crowd party, I was struck by the realization that this "movement" was not going to unfold as I had expected and hoped. That truth began to spread in my heart until I felt nauseous and weak. I needed to find a place to lie down before I became a medical casualty myself. I heard a voice speak clearly in my mind: "To have peace on Earth, you must first have peace within yourself."

My expectations were shattered. I closed my eyes and took a brief nap. As I drifted off, I thought to myself, *What is inner peace?* The voice didn't answer.

How does a human being with inner peace behave? Why would this be necessary for *world peace*?

During my first summer in California, my brother had accrued some time off from his job, so we took an eleven-thousand-mile trip around the US and Canada, driving and exploring from the West Coast to the East Coast. We camped and visited family and friends along the way. Somewhere on our road trip in that sweet little Datsun 240Z, we decided that our bond as brother and sister was more important than our differences. I was twenty at the time, and my brother was twenty-six. I marvel at how different we were in many ways, but somehow, we knew the love that bound us as brother and sister. Even though we had different religious and spiritual beliefs, we recognized that love was the main and only ingredient in our family. That was a master class in truth.

We made a pact to do better than our parents did in their marriage and childrearing efforts. We had our share of arguments during the trip, but we returned home to California with our relationship not only intact but also strengthened.

I have heard it said many times in my life that "Love is the *only* question, and love is the *only* answer." Earlier in my life, I thought this was somewhat "airy-fairy," but I have come to realize that it most definitely is not.

I left California a year and a half later to move back into my mother's apartment in Pennsylvania. During this time in my life, I experimented with drugs, smoking pot, and tripping on acid and mushrooms. Everyone was so casual about it. Injecting drugs was as commonplace as having a beer at a party is today. I noticed many of my friends trying heroin, only to become seriously addicted. I never tried heroine, but my boyfriend Hutch and I did try cocaine. The rush from cocaine was so euphoric, and the crash was so horrendous, that it scared me tremendously. Consequently, I decided not to do drugs of any kind again, but the memory of the "rush" haunted me. It was then that I began to consider that there might be a way to achieve a "higher" state of consciousness naturally.

One day, I ran into an old high school friend who radiated an impressive sense of contentment. His eyes were clear, and they radiated peace. His new persona was such a striking departure from the person I had known! "I have found peace!" he said with excitement. "It is *within* you!"

"Peace is within you?" That message came to me again. My friend mentioned that he had become a devotee of a guru. He had undergone an initiation, given up all his material possessions, stopped using drugs, adopted a vegetarian diet, and practiced meditation for two hours a day.

Good Lord! I thought. I honestly couldn't make sense of his words, but the "vibe" emanating from him struck a powerful chord in me. I was aware of Americans who had traveled to

India to "find" a guru, and I was starting to wonder if I should do the same. Until that point in my life, I dealt with crushed expectations—my happy family shattered by divorce, my heart broken by my boyfriend, and the hopes and expectations of the hippie movement derailed by drugs. My friend suggested that I read a book that had just been published, called *Be Here Now* by Ram Dass.

I sat on my mattress on the bedroom floor, with cotton Indian blankets pinned up to the ceiling to create a Bedouin tent effect, and large throw pillows scattered across the floor. I lit candles and incense, reading the book from cover to cover, only stopping to eat. "My God, this is *it*!"

Ram Dass described his profound transformation through his devotion, love, service, and surrender to the teachings of his guru, Neem Karoli Baba. Although it was foreign to my Christian upbringing, it felt real and tangible to me. *Maybe,* I thought, *this is what it was like for Jesus's followers during his lifetime.* Even if Jesus were to return, I couldn't imagine that Christians would ever agree on this person, even if he per-formed miracles. Cynically, I mused, *The press would crucify him! Maybe I should stick with finding a guru!* Every word writ-ten in *Be Here Now* ignited a fire in my belly. Finally, I had discovered a way to achieve inner peace that resonated with me.

"I think we should check out this introductory program offered by the guru's devotional community in Philadelphia, don't you?" I casually suggested to my friend Angela. We had been friends since eighth grade.

We exchanged glances for a moment before she said, "Sure. Yeah, it looks interesting."

On the evening of the program, I was sitting in a friend's apartment before heading out to the event when everyone decided to shoot up some "smack" (a slang term for heroin). They asked if I wanted to join them. I hesitated for a moment but ultimately turned them down and went to the guru's program as planned. In retrospect, I realize that this was a decisive moment that powerfully changed the course of my life.

After attending the introductory program, I decided to join Guru Maharaji's devotional community and prepare for initiation. The guru did not reside in the Philadelphia ashram but traveled from India to his ashrams in various locations. On July 2, 1972, in the ashram in New York City, one of the Mahatmas from India, a devotee of Guru Maharaji, deemed me ready to receive my initiation.

When I first met Maharaji, he was fifteen years old, six years younger than I was. He was referred to as a "guru," a spiritual teacher who imparted initiation to show one the light within. Through the practice of knowledge, he was going to show me that peace is within. That is exactly what I was looking for! Honestly, it felt very authentic to me. I saw something in his devotees' eyes. After the disappointment I had felt from the peace movement and the message I received while at the peace rally in Washington, DC, I felt deeply compelled to explore this, and I didn't have to go to India!

On that day, a group of us sat on a carpeted floor for hours, listening to a sacred discourse. The Mahatma's discourse posed only one question to us: "Who do you think God is?" We all held different ideas about God. The Mahatma said, "You all believe in God, but you don't truly *know* God. Now, you're going to witness God."

I had never considered that there was a difference between believing in God and knowing God. *Maybe if I truly get to know God, I won't be so angry with him*, I thought. *Maybe I will gain a different perspective.*

I realized that, in truth, my relationship with God was quite abstract, and my internal relationship with God fell within the father–daughter spectrum. The Mahatma explained to us that each of our experiences would be distinct.

I was the last person in the room to experience initiation, which, in the best way I can describe it, was a transfer of energy that completely shifted my consciousness. In a book, Carlos Castaneda describes his teacher, a Mexican shaman, slapping him hard on a certain spot on his back and completely shifting his consciousness. I didn't receive a "back slap," but the initiation experience shifted my consciousness instantly.

My third eye opened, and I felt my soul or spirit shoot through a short red tunnel and out of my body. I experienced such euphoric feelings while exiting my body that I had a fleeting thought about why using drugs can be so addictive. That momentary euphoria reminds us of returning to our spiritual home.

In space, I felt the stars. My being was immense. It was utter, complete peace, and I sensed a loving presence. I realized in that moment that I was one with God, not separate or apart but unified. I instantly understood who I truly was and where I came from—that I was part of everything. I was home.

Then, *boom!* Someone turned on the lights. *I'm not finished!* I thought. *I want to stay outside my body!* I was home. The love, the wholeness! What were they thinking, turning on the lights?

The Mahatma moved around the room, asking everyone to share what they had experienced. I listened intently, eager to find some validation for what had happened to me. Yet, not a single person in that room described anything like it. As the last one to speak, I felt like I was about to explode by the time the Mahatma reached me. Surely, I thought, he would stand up, embrace me, and sing my praises for being a fully realized being. Surely, he would.

When the Mahatma approached me, he said, "And, dear sister, what was your experience?" Catching my breath, I shared all of it. "That's nice," he said, nodding his head. Then, he went on to teach us how to meditate.

Nice? *That's nice?* I thought. Honestly, I wanted to crawl up to the front and strangle him. But by the end of our session, I didn't feel as much of a need for someone else to verify what had happened to me. I *knew* I had been awakened. Suddenly, I felt "grown up." I could no longer whine and complain about God, Jesus, and peace. I had gone in search of myself, and by God, I had found what I was looking for.

But did I make peace with God? No, the thought never occurred to me. I now knew this place of clarity and vibrational alignment with God, Creation, and Source, but I was more comfortable living in what is often referred to as the illusion, which carried with it many lessons.

You might think, *That's it! At nearly twenty-one years old, this woman could live her life in perfect peace and harmony.* Well, not exactly. Even after receiving such a magnificent gift, I left the room wishing to return to that familiar, comfortable state of ignorance. *Now, this is not how I expected to feel.*

When my time there ended, I walked down the steps to the ground floor to find my boyfriend, Hutch, waiting for me. He studied my face. "So, how was it? Are you enlightened?" I don't remember what I said, but in that moment, I wanted to go to a party and get stoned. I wanted to do something that felt "normal." Can you imagine, having had such a life-altering experience, and I suddenly wanted to go back to that familiar place of not knowing . . . to the pain and emptiness?

We went to dinner at a restaurant in New York with a friend, and I ordered a grilled cheese sandwich since I was officially a vegetarian. While we were in the restaurant, the room became exceptionally illuminated by an unusual light. I closed my eyes and took a deep breath. Deep within my solar plexus, I felt something akin to a seed, and with it, I experienced a profound, intoxicating sense of peace. I realized that the practices I had just learned were meant to nurture that seed, to expand my consciousness and the light within. I was beginning to experience the simple axiom "Peace is within."

Interestingly, a friend of Hutch's who joined us for dinner that evening mentioned he was leaving for India the next day to begin his spiritual journey in search of inner peace and possibly a guru! I gazed into his face, unable to articulate my thoughts, but I pondered, *Wow. I discovered the God within on 83rd Street in New York City! I didn't have to go to India to find my guru.*

I had always felt that my relationship with my guru was unconventional since I was not living in his ashram. I only saw him closely when I was in a queue walking through to receive his "darshan" (bowing and kissing his feet). Those moments always opened and touched my heart, but I never felt a deep personal connection with him, as I imagined others must have who lived and worked closer to him. I was just one of many thousands of followers. I expected that my path to enlightenment would be less profound because I chose not to stay in the ashram.

Then, one day, I received a hastily written letter from my friend Deana, along with a round-trip ticket from Philadelphia to Miami. There was a program with the guru coming up, and I didn't have the money to attend. As it so happened, one of her friends who had purchased the ticket ended up staying in Miami and was unable to get her money back for the round-trip ticket. She asked Deana if she knew anyone who lived in Philadelphia who could use the ticket! It seemed divinely ordained that I attend that particular program, as I was the only devotee she knew living in Pennsylvania.

The day of the program, I was tasked with taking Deana's car to pick up the cheese pizza we had ordered for dinner. On the way home, I glanced over at the pizza box sitting on the car seat and spotted a cockroach—the small variety, not the big honking palmetto bugs that live in the South. (God is merciful!) Nevertheless, I completely freaked out and almost ran off the road while trying to slip my flip-flop off to bludgeon the little bugger.

I ended up crushing the top of the box in the process.

"Oh my God, girl, get a grip!" I told myself. "You're going to cause a car accident."

The only thing that provided me with a small modicum of composure was knowing that Deana's husband, Pat, had just been accepted into a graduate program at Yale University, and they had no extra money to deal with a wrecked car! Gripping the wheel with both hands and clutching the flip-flop in my right hand, breath by breath, I made it back to their apartment.

"What the hell happened to the pizza box?" Deana asked when I arrived at my destination. "Was it like that when you picked it up?"

I recounted the story of the cockroach, mindful that my voice was barely holding back hysteria. "I don't think I got it. I think it's still in the car!"

The conversation shifted to other topics, but I silently continued my scientific analysis of how that cockroach was going to die. I was so utterly terrified at the thought of getting into that car again with a cockroach scurrying around that I must have started babbling to the point where Deana turned to me in exasperation and said, "Enough about the freaking cockroach already."

I could ask Deana for some bug spray, but I knew that might piss her off. So, I began to think about how it was well over a hundred degrees in that car. I had rolled up all the windows, so surely *nothing* could survive in that heat. Maybe in my frantic panic, I had injured it, and it was going to die.

When we got back into the car to go to the guru's program, I slipped off my sandal and quietly held it at the ready. My mind was still completely consumed by the terror of that little cockroach. I prayed it did not make an appearance, as I knew I might come apart.

I sat way in the back of the bleachers, and there were about five thousand people at the program that evening. But when Maharaji came out onstage, my heart leaped with joy, and I completely forgot about my cockroach problem.

Maharaji began his evening discourse with a discussion on how fear can completely take over the mind. "For instance," he said, "consider something like a cockroach. It's amazing how a little bug like that can evoke such great fear! Their scurrying about is truly terrifying, and even if you squash them with your shoe, they still seem to survive. They can endure in the harshest conditions. You can place them in a closed jar without food or water, and they can survive a very long time. Even locked in a hot car with the windows closed, they still survive!"

Everyone in the audience laughed at this amusing way to start his satsang, but Maharaji's words imploded into my cells. I began to laugh so hard at myself that I caused a scene with my neighbors. I couldn't help it. I completely lost my fear in the sheer bliss of laughter. That was my moment, sitting in an audience with five thousand other devotees, when I felt a deeply personal connection with my guru.

Incorporating the practices of devotion, meditation, and service into my daily life proved to be quite challenging. I quickly recognized the value of going to India to live in an ashram removed from everyday life for months or even years.

The greatest struggle was the feeling that I was never doing "it" right. There was a subtle, critical voice that lingered, always present. Despite that, it was a great time in my life. I was healthy, happy, and lighthearted, for the most part. I loved the friends I made in the devotional community, but I still expected that I would never become truly enlightened.

In that moment of my initiation, when my third eye opened and I went through a red light, experiencing oneness with the Universe, being engulfed in blackness and seeing the stars represented a profound energetic shift. The love I felt was immense, coupled with a deep remembering that made me want to stay in this state. (I have read similar experiences from others describing near-death experiences.) This was a lot to reconcile despite the many hours of holy discourse I had absorbed. My ego quickly took over, as its role was to protect, and self-doubt crept in. I wondered why no one else had experienced or described this, not even my friend who had accompanied me, or the guy in front who sat in rigid meditation for several hours before the Mahatma began. With no one to talk to about this, I quietly soldiered on, plagued by self-doubt.

How do you process something of that magnitude that occurred during my initiation at twenty-one? Here I was, reading about inner peace and higher states of consciousness while experiencing altered states of consciousness to some degree through psychedelics. This resonated deeply with me. To quote Denise Linn, "The soul loves the truth." I reflected on how I sought to reconcile the *experience* of the Divine and Source energy. At that time, I followed the guru, believing that being a devotee was the pathway to enlightenment and the only way to achieve it. You had to follow this guru and devote every waking moment to the practices of meditation, service, and satsang (listening to holy discourse). I once called a friend who had just returned from a long sea voyage as a cook and told her she was "sailing on the wrong ocean and that there was an ocean of peace inside her." I was very enthusiastic, so sure *this* was it! I had found the holy grail of experiencing peace within. Every other pathway was null and void; this was the *only* way it could work. (Definitely something bleeding through from my Christian upbringing.)

There was nothing wrong with this way of life; it was a common practice among the people of India, much like the various branches and practices of Christian religions. However, I had never experienced anything like that in my spiritual journey, and I was very zealous when sharing it with my friends.

It was during this practice that I truly began to grasp the concept of reincarnation. Experiencing the connection and vastness of my being in that moment of *remembrance*, I realized I was not separate but part of everything. I acknowledged that I had lived other lifetimes, yet I didn't give it much thought at the time. I still had much to learn.

While integrating this new practice into my life, I felt like I was living in two worlds. Although the construct of service, holy discourse, and meditation served as the foundation for merging my two worlds, I found it a struggle and kept defaulting to the construct of Christianity in some form.

The following story effectively illustrates this point . . .

Once, when I was in Maui with my family, we went out with a group for a few hours of snorkeling in an area offshore by a remnant of a volcano protruding above the surface of the ocean. It is a lovely and well-known spot as the underwater reefs around it are rich with marine life.

I was somewhat isolated from the group, closer to the spot where the ruins emerged from the water. Suddenly, I heard the whales singing their songs, echoing off the curved surface of the underwater volcano. OMG, they were in the area! I panicked and lifted my head out of the water, but I couldn't see any above or within my field of vision below the waterline. I put my head back in the water, and once again, this loud, vibrational chorus filled my ears. I did this several times because I couldn't believe what was happening. Eventually, I calmed down from my fear of large whales being nearby (in reality, they weren't that close) and floated while listening. The vibration resonated deep within my body and into my heart; I started to sob as I raised my head out of the water to see where I was. Never in my life have I experienced anything so loving and penetrating; it truly changed my vibration. Just dipping my head into the water brought about this life-changing experience. In many ways, this was my moment of awakening. Head in the water, I experienced the whale song; head out, nothing.

CHAPTER 3

A Lesson in Forgiveness

"To err is human, to forgive, divine."

—ALEXANDER POPE

One evening, while I sat on my mattress working on a new song on my guitar, Alex came over to visit. He praised my song, and we decided to walk up to the Hill (the same place I went to talk to God and Jesus). We sat for a while and chatted under my favorite tree. Then, out of the blue, Alex leaned in and kissed me. We were both surprised by this sudden shift in the landscape of our friendship.

Hutch and I had already parted ways. My new life of devotion and meditation was not meant for him. Alex had battled heroin addiction, so I encouraged him to visit the guru to become initiated into the devotional practices of meditation, service, and satsang (Sanskrit for "being with the truth"). From my own experience, I understood that the inner peace stemming from the bond between guru and devotee is incredibly powerful. I was convinced that this loving and healing relationship would aid in curing Alex's addiction.

After he began practicing meditation, his mother noticed a difference in him. "He looks more at peace than I've ever seen him!" she said to me, tears in her eyes. This was a woman who did not mince words. She had a Catholic upbringing, a sharp tongue, Irish humor, and great intelligence. She had also raised eleven children. Because of the progress she observed in Alex, she even joined us at the ashram several times to hear holy discourse. Alex had struggled with severe behavioral issues as a child, so his parents hoped he had reached a turning point in his life.

How little I knew then about the power of opiate addiction. Despite his spiritual awakening, Alex continued to struggle with heroin use. Consequently, his father bought him a ticket to Florida so Alex could stay with his brother, who was working there for the winter. I decided to leave my job to join him for a few months. We lived in a campsite we shared with five other friends.

One morning, I was the last to awaken. When I joined everyone else, Alex's brother handed me a piece of paper. "This is for you." I tried to search his eyes for clues about the note, but he avoided my gaze. That told me everything I needed to know: Alex had left without saying a word to hitchhike back up North.

How could he do that to me? I took my hurt and confusion for a walk and sat by the water. It was so early in the morning that the sun wasn't even fully up yet. I remembered my past heartbreaks—the suffering I had experienced, the deadness—and I hoped there was a way to avoid that horrible pain this time. I expected that with spiritual enlightenment, I would no longer feel the agony of abandonment and discomfort I was enduring. Soon, the blazing orb of the sun rose over the horizon, and my heart began to lift with it. A tremendous sense of peace started to spread from my heart, filling my entire being, until I radiated true bliss. It seemed vital for me to acknowledge and feel my emotions and sadness, yet I did not have to become submerged in their depths until I could no longer reasonably function.

My girlfriend arrived to see if she could offer some comfort. I turned away from the sunrise to watch her approach, smiling broadly. "The sun has risen!" I exclaimed. Suddenly, I felt certain: "I don't have to be swallowed by the abyss of heartbreak any longer—not ever!"

Ah . . . the naiveté of youth!

My friend and I made plans to drive back North, but the day before, we had one last romp on the beach with the rest of the group. I was nursing an infection in my foot, so I sat on a towel alone and watched my friends play in the surf. A tall, lanky young man with sandy brown hair approached me several times, trying to spark a conversation. He wasn't overly aggressive, but he bothered me repeatedly—so much so that I decided to join my friends in the water despite my foot injury.

Later that evening, I visited a friend and walked back to the campsite alone. A car pulled up next to me in the oncoming traffic lane. I recognized the driver as the same man who had bothered me on the beach. I stood under a bright streetlight as we exchanged greetings. Another man exited the passenger side and approached me aggressively. As he attempted to grab me, a wave of shock coursed through my body when I turned my back to him. We struggled, and I knew I had to "turn off my mind." I called out to my guru for help. In that split second, the man opened the back-seat door and nearly managed to force me inside.

I spread my hands on the car and suddenly felt a great surge of energy flowing in through the top of my head. It felt soft, golden in color, almost liquid, and full of love. As it filled my being, everything grew quiet, slipping into slow motion, and I became very calm. Turning toward the man, I said, "Hey, man, stop fighting me. I'll get in the car." He relaxed his grip, allowing me to turn and face him. I looked into his eyes. Under the glow of the streetlamp, I could see there was no light in his eyes—they were so dark and eerie. I could feel the emptiness of his soul, and I knew one thing for sure in that moment: his intention was to kill me.

I also became aware of my left hand rising to strike him. Accompanying my hand, emanating from this immense presence of love that enveloped my body, was the unspoken realization that this stranger—even though I was sure he intended to kill me—was my brother. He wasn't a biological brother, of course, but a brother in the human race. I gazed into his eyes, and with no fear or hatred—just love—I struck him with such force that he soared through the air to my right. "Run!" I heard a voice in my head shout.

Thankfully, the driver never got out of the car.

I ran as fast as I could back to our campsite. Bursting through the camper door and gasping for breath, I screamed, "That guy! That guy! That guy on the beach!" In the time it took to run from the car to the campsite, I had become unhinged and hysterical.

"Wendy, what the hell are you talking about? What guy? Where were you?" They were worried sick about me, but I wasn't making any sense. When they finally managed to calm me down enough to explain what happened, I chose to omit the "otherworldly" part of my experience.

My friends Boz and Mac gathered information from my description and went in search of the car. No one even thought to call the police, opting instead for some form of vigilante action. Of course, none of us realized how dangerous this situation could have become if they had encountered the assailants, but we were all too young to know any better.

For many years, I pushed that incident out of my mind. When I finally began to process the attack, all I could think about was that I might have saved someone's life if I had stayed in town and reported it. Did they ever find a murder victim? I felt guilt and anger toward myself. I was too young to embrace the grace and meaning of what had happened to me. All I managed at that point was to internalize that guilt.

In the late 1980s, however, an experience brought me back to the time of the attack. This experience deepened my understanding of what had happened to me, and I felt a healing I didn't even know I needed. My brother and his family were living in a lovely, quaint community outside Amsterdam in the Netherlands. His company had sent him to Europe to work for a few years, so my new boyfriend and I decided to visit.

My sister-in-law wanted to take us to a museum in Haarlem, where she had volunteered as an English tour guide. We arrived at a slightly crooked house near the town center that was three stories high and only as wide as a small room. This house had belonged to the ten Boom family, whose story gained worldwide notoriety for their work during World War II as part of the Dutch underground during the Nazi occupation of Holland. A deeply Christian family, the ten Booms worked tirelessly to help the Jews.

Installed in Corrie ten Boom's room, there was an ingenious false wall that the Nazis remarkably never discovered. The story of their family's life, work, eventual betrayal, and internment in a concentration camp is documented in Corrie's book *The Hiding Place*, which she coauthored with John and Elizabeth Sherrill, as well as in a film produced by evangelical minister Billy Graham. This tour profoundly affected me, prompting me to purchase the book at the museum and begin reading it immediately.

As I read the story, I didn't feel like I was thousands of miles away. I felt as though I were in the very rooms where the courageous struggle against Hitler's Nazi Germany occurred. There was a particular passage toward the end of the book that shook me to my core. Corrie ten Boom was preaching in a church in Munich after the war. She had come to believe that forgiveness was the only path to truly healing the devastation of the Holocaust.

Corrie shared with the congregation her own struggles with forgiveness. "It was at a church service in Munich that I saw him, the former S.S. man who had stood guard at the shower room door in the processing center at Ravensbruck. He was the first of our actual jailers that I had seen since that time. And suddenly it was all there—the roomful of mocking men, the heaps of clothing, [Corrie's sister] Betsie's pain-blanched face. He came up to me as the church was emptying, beaming and bowing. 'How grateful I am for your message, Fraulein,' he said. 'To think that, as you say, He has washed my sins away!' His hand was thrust out to shake mine. And I, who had preached so often to the people in Bloemendaal the need to forgive, kept my hand at my side. Even as the angry, vengeful thoughts boiled through me, I saw the sin of them. Jesus Christ had died for this man; was I going to ask for more? *Lord Jesus*, I prayed, *forgive me, and help me to forgive him*. I tried to smile. I struggled to raise my hand. I could not. I felt nothing, not the slightest spark of warmth or charity. And so again, I breathed a silent prayer. *Jesus, I cannot forgive him. Give me Your forgiveness.* As I took his hand, the most incredible thing happened. From my shoulder along my arm and through my hand, a current seemed to pass from me to him, while into my heart sprang a love for this stranger that almost overwhelmed me. And so I discovered that it is not upon our forgiveness any more than on our goodness that the world's healing hinges, but on His. When He tells us to love our enemies, He gives, along with the command, the love itself."

I sobbed as I read that passage. The full implications of my attack rushed back in a sudden flood of emotion. In my moment of need, I called out to my guru by name. I didn't cry out for Jesus like Corrie, but I had a very similar experience. Lo and behold, perhaps God didn't care or take it personally! Corrie was so right—to forgive is divine.

Such a lesson here . . .

Calling out to my guru for help, just inches away from my attacker's face and staring into his eyes, I was acutely aware of his desire to kill me. I felt energy flowing through my body from the top of my head, accompanied by a light radiating with love. This divine experience—of physically striking someone while feeling the emotion of love for my brother as time slowed down—was grace.

I don't intend to minimize the absolute horrors of the Holocaust while sharing the awakening I experienced from reading this passage by Corrie ten Boom. Instead, I reflect on the profound lesson that it is possible to find oneself in a moment filled with hatred and fear, and yet, when a prayer is sent out for help, it is answered.

Regardless of the name you choose, you are never denied.

I paused for a moment to reflect on the state of the world and my country, which seem so divided by insurmountable differences, ideologies, and beliefs. Sometimes, I hesitate to confront my anger or hatred; I don't want to let it go—it feels so justified! However, I seek help, just as I did that day. Soon, my experience begins to soften, and I realize that, if I am willing, the light of greater understanding will arrive.

CHAPTER 4

Meth and Violence

"If you understand, things are just as they are; if you do not understand, things are just as they are."

—ZEN PROVERB

When I returned to Pennsylvania, Alex was there to greet me. *Surprise . . .*

He explained why he had left Florida so abruptly. I no longer remember what he said, but I must have been fine with the explanation. Our relationship resumed, and we decided to live together. One day, after making love, Alex caressed my abdomen and posed a question. "Why don't we have a baby?"

Why not, indeed?

There were profound individual psychological issues at play for each of us, independent of one another. In my case, my parents had gone through a horrendous divorce, and I became a pawn for my mother's deep anger and hurt. She often used me in an attempt to wound my father, who had left their marriage for another woman. The three of them—my mother, father, and the other woman—created a force to be reckoned with in their dramas. I was far too young to comprehend what was happening, but needless to say, marriage was not an institution I felt compelled to embrace.

I continued to practice meditation sporadically, which kept me connected to a deeply fulfilling spiritual program. However, it did not influence my practical, day-to-day decisions at that time. I reasoned that since Alex and I weren't living in an ashram and were, therefore, not celibate, we would leave it to the fates. If I got pregnant, it was meant to be. Within ten months of that day, the fates took over, and I found out I was pregnant.

We had already moved back to Florida, and life seemed good. Alex had become loving and attentive, and we both had jobs. However, not long after we found out we were expecting a baby, things began to change.

Alex approached me one day with a sheepish grin on his face and blurted out, "I have a venereal disease, and you need to get checked out."

"What?!" I was unable to grasp the full impact of his words.

Alex repeated, "I have contracted a venereal disease from someone at work that I've been having sex with."

"You fucking cheat! How could you jeopardize the baby and me like that? You fucking insensitive bastard!"

I felt trapped and betrayed beyond words. *Oh, dear God, what have I done?* I wondered. It was a rude awakening, but at least the doctor confirmed that I was okay, as was the baby. Well, I was all right physically, anyway.

Alex seemed so nonplussed about the whole episode, which raised a few alarm bells, but I wanted so much to believe everything would be "just fine" and that the birth of our baby would bring us closer together. At least, I anticipated that would happen.

We decided to move out West before the baby was born. Alex left for a month to find us a place to live. He looked in California and then in Colorado because we had a close mutual friend living near the Denver area. There was an active devotional community in Denver. Alex soon found an apartment there, and although I had strong misgivings about joining him, he convinced me once again that we would be okay, which was desperately what I wanted to believe.

In our new apartment building, we were surrounded by people who were part of the guru's devotional community. Therefore, I assumed this would help me keep my life together. However, if you remove the "f" from "life," you get "lie."

Several deeply disturbing events occurred around the time of my son Jamie's birth. While in my ninth month of pregnancy, Alex and I met a young architect who had recently moved into the apartment upstairs and was not part of the devotional community. He was handicapped and had to get around on crutches. He enlisted my help to buy items for his apartment, such as sheets, towels, dishes, and rugs. He kindly bought similar items for us as well while shopping with me, knowing we were strapped financially.

After Jamie was born, he even came to the hospital and paid our bill! He was very kind and generous. However, one day, Alex returned home from work to find unmarked cars surrounding our building, which he suspected might belong to federal agents. Alex had some outstanding warrants, but nothing that would provoke such a response from the federal government. We decided that I should go see what was happening. Alex suggested I start with our friend, the "architect." It turned out he was in the process of being arrested by the agents. I stared at him in shock as I watched him stand up without his crutches.

One of the agents noticed my reaction. "He is not crippled; nor is he an architect."

Holding my newborn baby in my arms, I began to cry. "He has been so kind to us. He came to visit me in the hospital and covered our hospital bill after my delivery!"

"Well," the agent explained, "he's suspected of robbing banks in several nearby states. I don't think the tellers who had guns held to their heads are feeling particularly kindly toward him."

After our generous neighbor was taken away, I discovered that he had given Alex some cash, so I immediately brought it to the agents.

"Well, lady, this is your lucky day. None of the serial numbers on these bills correspond with the serial numbers from the stolen money. He must have believed he was some kind of Robin Hood character, stealing money to help the poor."

He had also given money to other people in our building, but none of it matched the stolen bills. We were all speechless.

As I was leaving the architect's apartment, the agent informed me that the man had left everything in his apartment to us and several other families.

Another incident occurred just before I gave birth to Jamie.

My first boyfriend, William, was living in a mountain community near Boulder with his girlfriend. William was the one who convinced Alex to move to Denver, and he was also a heroin user. Whenever he and Alex got together, they caused serious mayhem and epic crises. I always had misgivings about their activities, and for good reason, but I agreed to visit William and his girlfriend in the mountains for the weekend.

On the second night of our visit, Alex and I were hanging out with some neighbors, peacefully relaxing and watching television, when three men burst through the open patio door. They were skinny, poorly dressed, and had unkempt long hair. They appeared to be very hyped up on meth. Before I could even grasp what was happening, there was a gun to my head.

"Nobody move!" a young man shouted, wildly waving a gun and poking it against my head.

"We're looking for Bear and Hawk, and we were told they are here!"

"Bear" was William. The other two guys searched the place and quickly found William naked in bed with his girlfriend. They grabbed his arm and dragged him into the living room.

"Where's Hawk?" they shouted in a dissonant chorus. "You better fucking tell us right now, or we're going to start hurting people!"

I silently glanced in Alex's direction and noticed that his slightly lazy left eye had drifted inward within its socket. I had learned that this was always a sign of extreme stress or fear.

Jesus Christ!! I thought to myself. *What the hell have William and Alex done to these men? They're going to kill us all!*

Alex and William had "gone out to the store" the night

before and had been away for a long time. I sensed something was wrong, but I didn't want to admit it had anything to do with drugs. Now, I had a gun to my head that forced me to snap out of my denial quickly.

"Come on!" one of the men shouted as he signaled for everyone but William to pile into the bathroom. Just before shutting the door, he handed us a joint. The four of us stared at each other in shock and silence. A joint? Really?

They proceeded to tie William up, after which they subjected him to a terrible beating while trying to get him to tell them where they could find Hawk (aka Alex) and the drugs they had stolen the previous evening. For some reason, they had apparently recognized William's voice, but not Alex's.

In a desperate attempt to get them to stop beating William, I cried out through the bathroom door, "Please, please stop! For God's sake, you're causing me to have labor pains. It's hurting the baby!"

They paused for a moment, took me out of the bathroom, and sat me down in the bedroom. Then, they started beating William again. When they determined that he wasn't going to tell them where they could find Hawk or their drugs, they proceeded to tear the house apart, looking for the drugs themselves. What I learned is that William and Alex had robbed them in a similar manner the previous evening. Someone ratted them out, so these guys came for their revenge.

I don't remember if the men found what they were looking for, but they eventually left. William was badly beaten but did not want to go to the hospital or call the police.

When Alex entered the bedroom, I glared at him. "I don't want to be with you anymore," I said matter-of-factly. "It's over."

I left the room to join the others in an adjacent family room. The small, modest home had been ransacked. They had even attempted to tear out the stove in search of their drugs. We were all deeply shaken, having never witnessed such manic craziness except on television.

In the meantime, Alex took a knife from the kitchen to protect himself in case the guys returned and carried it into the bedroom, where he began shredding the few clothes I had brought to Colorado with me. When he returned to the family room, he looked like a wild dog and started hitting me.

"What the fuck are you doing, man?!" William screamed as he jumped up from his seat and tackled Alex to the floor. Despite being badly bruised, William appeared determined to get Alex to calm down.

We all walked over to a neighbor's house to spend the night on their floor. The next morning, I felt numb and didn't want to return to our apartment in Denver with Alex. I needed some time to think.

It so happened that an old high school boyfriend of mine, Roddy, lived just outside of Denver. He was a kind and wonderful man, and he allowed me to stay in the house he shared with several people, including his fiancée. Unfortunately, Roddy's roommates weren't happy with the arrangement and made it very clear that I wasn't welcome to stay.

Therefore, when Alex came over to speak with me, apologizing and swearing that he would never do drugs or hit me again, I felt I had no choice but to go with him. I was nearing my due date at that point, had no money, and nowhere else to turn. I still wanted desperately to believe Alex, so I returned to our apartment. Everything settled down for a few weeks as Alex tried to keep his promise. I knew he wanted to believe everything would be fine as much as I did, but I could also sense him struggling with his demons.

Alex was a deep thinker; he felt things in this world and understood spiritual ideals far more than I did. This is what attracted me to him as a friend in the first place. He always took me on spiritual journeys, whether with acid or pot, and these experiences—whether on his motorcycle or during walks in the woods—always nourished my soul. We laughed a lot. He introduced me to so many concepts about people's "vibrations" that I found him very wise. Later, when we became lovers, I also realized he was an exquisite sexual partner.

Alex was the third child in a Catholic family of eleven siblings with Irish and Italian heritage. He spent much of his early teenage years in institutions known as "reformatories" for his education. He faced numerous behavioral issues, and this environment seemed to provide him with some success. Alex shared with me that there was one priest in particular who managed to connect with and help him. In hindsight, I suspect that Alex had significant learning disabilities; however, these various childhood experiences also contributed to his difficulties.

One day, when I was seventeen, years before we became lovers, Alex showed up at my door. As I opened it, he looked at me and said, "I am a father." I stood there with my mouth open, thinking we were going for a motorcycle ride. His young girlfriend at the time, who was still in high school, had somehow denied her pregnancy and woke up in the middle of the night at her parents' house, believing she had to go to the bathroom but was actually in active labor and, much to her mother's horror, gave birth to a small baby boy. Alex came in and sat down, appearing shell-shocked. All I could manage to say was, "Oh, wow . . ."

He sold his motorcycle, they got married, and lived in a third-floor apartment at his parents' home. I'm not sure if this was the impetus for him to start using heroin.

The marriage fell apart within two years.

I went into labor on a beautiful fall day.

I endured a long and difficult delivery. My baby was in a breech position, and my amniotic sac broke, resulting in a "dry birth." But after many hours, Jamie entered this world.

Afterward, I felt as if I had given birth to Thor, the God of Thunder, and I went into shock, experiencing a high fever for a while. Of course, I eventually got better and was able to go home with Jamie. Still in denial, I wanted to believe that with the baby finally in front of him, Alex would magically transform into a great dad and settle into normalcy. After all, Alex wanted this baby as much as I did.

Not long after Jamie's birth, the doorbell rang, and when I opened the door—much to my surprise—I found my Uncle Ben with his new wife, who is twenty-five years his junior, beaming at me, clearly delighted to have found me. I didn't even know my uncle was in Colorado! I learned that he had moved to Boulder from New England in hopes of improving his wife's severe asthma.

I was overjoyed to see anyone from my family, as my immediate family was so distraught by my decision to have a baby out of wedlock that they made it clear they wanted nothing to do with me, Alex, or even the baby. I have to say, though, that I was a college dropout, following some young guru, my boyfriend was a heroin addict who had been in and out of prison (still with a warrant out for his arrest), and here I was, bringing a child into this world. It looked bad because it was bad. But these were my choices at the time.

Uncle Ben and his wife took me out to dinner with the new baby. *This feels so lovely and normal*, I thought. Uncle Ben had always made me feel special and never treated me like the "loser" I felt I was. He had a great deal of intelligence and charm. He was well-educated, with a law degree from Yale, and he had both made and spent a lot of money. The timing of his arrival in my life was a godsend.

In light of everything I had been experiencing, coupled with an overwhelming sense of failure, I had shut down my spiritual growth without realizing how important it is to maintain it, especially during challenging times. When Uncle Ben dropped me off at my basement apartment, he said, "You're always welcome to stay with us, you know, if you ever need to. Also, have Alex come by my office tomorrow to see if we can sort out his outstanding warrant."

After some checking, Uncle Ben felt that Alex's warrant would only be executed if Alex was caught breaking the law again. It was clear that local Pennsylvania law enforcement wasn't expending any energy looking for him. This lightened our spirits, as we began to settle into a routine that finally felt somewhat stable. But stability is not part of an addict's world—at least, not for long.

To facilitate my delivery of Jamie, the doctor had to perform an episiotomy—an incision through the vaginal wall and perineum (the area between the vagina and the anus). The healing process was painful, and I wasn't supposed to have sex for at least six weeks. I didn't particularly want to have sex anyway, but Alex, of course, didn't care that I was still healing. "No!" I pleaded. "I'm still too sore!" He snapped and began hitting me when I tried to refuse him. Then, he raped me. He said he would be "gentle," but it hurt like hell. I was afraid, so it was easier to just give in and get through the painful intercourse.

Later that day, while I nursed my newborn child, I reflected on what Alex had done and began to accept the full gravity of my situation. Overcome with self-loathing and sadness, I looked into the trusting eyes of my son, with little tufts of white hair starting to emerge from his head. His legs grew chubbier by the day, and he was completely dependent on me. A silent, fierce warrior began to rise within my soul. I suddenly felt like a mother bear determined to protect her cub. I found the strength to do for Jamie what I could not do for myself.

I knew without any hesitation that I needed to leave Alex. I called my uncle and went to stay with him, taking only my clothes and things for the baby. His lovely home was my refuge while I made plans to return to Pennsylvania to stay with my mother.

Although my mother didn't like my life choices, she welcomed me into her apartment. Uncle Ben loaned me some money and also called my father and stepmother, Patricia, to tell them of my dire circumstances.

Ben was one of four boys born to my grandmother and grandfather. There was significant sibling rivalry in their family, particularly between Ben and my father. While my father was successful in the corporate world and worked hard, he always lived more modestly than his younger brother. The call from Ben about my problems must have been very humiliating for my father, and it certainly stirred the pot. When Ben put me on the phone, both Patricia and my father took the opportunity to chastise me for my abysmal life failures.

My father fell in love with Patricia after meeting her in a coffee shop near his office in downtown Philadelphia when I was eight and my brother was fourteen. At that point, he and my mother had been married for sixteen years when he asked for a divorce. I guess no one really went to marriage counseling in those days.

Patricia was very beautiful, smart, and successful in her career as a secretary to a company president. She was also creative and sewed much of her own clothing, curtains, and slipcovers, always keeping their home immaculate. I marveled at that during my visits.

After my father left our mother, our home fell into disrepair. Mom was so depressed that the house became filthy, the lawn was never mowed, and the gardens grew wild. There were rarely any clean clothes available. My mother wouldn't let me wash my clothes or even my hair. Most of the time, I looked like a street urchin. She was particularly careful to ensure I appeared disheveled when I visited my father.

Patricia would look at me with disgust and send me directly to the shower. My father and stepmother even took me clothes shopping so that I would have clean clothes to wear when we went out together. When I returned to my mother's in the evening, I had to leave the new clothes at my father's house and put my dirty clothes back on.

I admired many qualities in Patricia, but she also possessed a dark side. She was highly possessive of my father and often abusive and venomously critical of me. At times, she would turn on me in the middle of a conversation. "The biggest mistake I made in my life was marrying a man who had children." I always wondered what I had done to provoke her, but I think it was simply that I was my father's daughter from his first marriage.

Of course, what I did not understand was that she was a narcissist; she was full of jealousy and resentment at the slightest sign of love from my father and would gaslight me in a vicious way.

This is one of the reasons I felt so worthless as a kid. I wanted to be their child so that I could live in a clean house and have nice clothes. My father always seemed to love me dearly, but I learned early on that, in spite of his love, he was very cautious not to be overly affectionate with me when Patricia was around. The subtext for me was that keeping her happy was a way to make him happy. I was always on eggshells there.

Little Jamie and I settled into life with my mother in her two-bedroom apartment once we returned to Pennsylvania.

God bless her for taking us in. After I got a job, I sent my Uncle Ben money each month to pay off my plane ticket debt. I was unaware that my mother, who earned little from her job, as well as my father, also sent Ben money for my plane ticket! Ben took the money from all three of us and never mentioned it. He could be a scoundrel.

Meanwhile, Alex packed up the apartment in Colorado and drove back to Pennsylvania, where he stayed with his family. His large Irish-Italian Catholic family always made Jamie and me feel welcome—and they embraced him with open arms. However, Alex wasn't particularly interested in being a father; this behavior is not uncommon among those struggling with addiction.

One day, Alex showed up at my door. "Hey there," he said, shifting from one foot to the other. I quietly searched his face and found the familiar dilated pupils in his pale blue eyes. Without pretense, I shouted, "No more, Alex! No more! You're not going to see Jamie when you're high!" I slammed the door, and he left.

Eventually, I began to realize that I had been attempting to fix Alex and his problems, but I was ill-prepared for that task. In my efforts, I profoundly neglected my own issues. This realization stung, yet it also encouraged me to take responsibility for my actions and redirect my focus toward a more productive path.

I continued to practice meditation sporadically and listened to holy discourse from my guru, yet I remained in survival mode. Although I had only a part-time job, I found it challenging to care for my son while working. My childhood friends were finishing college, partying, and launching their careers. Fitting in was difficult. I struggled with the daily tasks of motherhood, but I loved Jamie deeply. I was resolute in my decision not to be a victim of life and committed to taking responsibility for my choices while striving to do better.

Despite all my struggles, unbeknownst to me at that time, Jamie's life had become my rudder. His birth was hardly an accident. Although I knew this truth deep within my soul, I found it difficult to reconcile it in my psyche.

I was in survival mode, though I didn't yet understand the gift of being that uncomfortable. Slowly it did push me into reconnecting with my spiritual community, journaling, meditation, and listening to discourse. In time I learned about making soul agreements prior to incarnation and was able to shed a lot of light on this time in my life.

One day when I was working as a vet tech, Alex came to see me. I hadn't seen him in a while, but it was good to catch up. He had a friend with him whom I did not recognize. On their way out, they helped themselves to the money in the cash box at the front desk. There were no clients waiting to be seen, so the girl who worked there was out getting lunch.

When she returned, she noticed that the cash in the cash box was missing. She informed the doctor, who was aware that some friends had just stopped by to see me. He was absolutely furious and reported it to the police. I knew that Alex and his friend had taken the money, and I was devastated. Although it was only a small amount—around fifty dollars—the doctor pressed charges, and I was grateful that I did not get fired.

Since Alex committed many legal infractions, he went to prison for a short time.

One day, as I was going into the prison with some other people to see an art exhibit by another inmate and an old boyfriend, Alex must have seen me through a window in the gym area. I looked over and saw him jumping up to get a glimpse of me walking up the steps.

As I left the exhibit and walked to my car, I suddenly heard this voice ring out from inside the building.

"Hey, Wendy! I'll make sure I pay you back the fifty dollars when I get out of here!" It was so eerie it sent chills up my spine. It scared the hell out of me.

A few months later, after riding my horse, I visited a friend's apartment to say hello; she lived down the hall from my mother and me. I opened the door, and there stood Alex. I froze.

I was uncertain about what would happen next. He quickly assured me that it was all his fault and that I had nothing to worry about. We could return to being friends.

In retrospect, that moment on the Hill—stomping around and demanding that God and Jesus tell me what the hell was going on—became the fertilizer that helped seeds of profound grace and self-awareness take root in my soul. Spirit didn't do the work for me; that's the "great gift" of feeling uncomfortable. I had to seek out and then enact the changes that better represent who I am and who I want to be. The truth is they hold the space for my growth with a love that can only be experienced and felt. As I fall down and get up, fall down and get up, over and over again, I can feel the extraordinary unconditional love that holds absolutely no judgment.

CHAPTER 5

Meeting Angelo

"What's wrong with knowing what you
know now and not knowing what you
don't know until later?"

—WINNIE THE POOH

While trying to rebuild my life in Pennsylvania, I felt I had a
foothold in two worlds: the divine realm expressed through my
meditation practice and devotion to my guru, and the everyday world of living, which I seemed only marginally capable of
managing.

I schlepped Jamie along with me to large gatherings where
Guru Maharaji spoke. Although I was going through the motions
and experiencing a few moments of connection, peace, and even
true bliss at times, I felt alone and out of sync with my friends
in the devotional community.

The Mahatmas spoke to us about the duality of the world—
darkness and light, good and bad, happy and sad, rich and
poor—the dual consciousness in which we were living. "Dear
brothers and sisters, you must continue to practice meditation, service, and listen to holy discourse. This will elevate you
beyond duality and bring your consciousness into the light and

oneness of bliss. True consciousness is one of eternal bliss, uniting with all that is. Sat chit anon."

I knew this to be true because I had experienced true consciousness—my true essence—during my initiation. In the presence of my guru, I felt an overwhelming sense of peace. Bringing these two different worlds together would be like a great merger, I thought. I wondered how my life might appear if I could blend and weave these parts together. I struggled with self-doubt, and it all seemed elusive, filled with "if onlys."

"Well, keep on trucking, girl," I said to myself. I usually worked two jobs to make ends meet, so I was too busy to spend much time pondering anything else.

My mother did the best she could. She loved her grandson and me, but after returning home from work each day, she would drink heavily. We lived in an apartment complex in a part of town that was regarded as somewhat of a slum. One of the bedrooms in the apartment was oversized, so I put up a divider to allow Jamie his own little space, separate from mine.

Although poor by any standard, my mother had a very regal air about her, speaking the "King's English" with even more precision when she was drinking. She was well-read, had knowledge of fine things, and possessed far more intelligence than she ever revealed.

Her father passed away when she was very young. Then the Depression hit, leaving her and her mother with very little money.

When my father left my mother, she was inconsolable with grief and rage. In her mind, that justified wrecking someone else's marriage. When I was ten, I awoke one night to strange "noises" coming from the living room, which was at the bottom of the stairs leading down to the first floor. They were unfamiliar sounds to me—heavy breathing, groans, and an unknown voice. I became afraid. After my father left, much of my life had become unpredictable. Every day hinged on my mother's mood. As I walked down the stairs, I called out to my mother and heard rustling. She met me halfway down and took me back to my room, telling me not to worry. She kissed me goodnight again, but I could smell the stench of alcohol and cigarettes on her breath.

One day while my mother was out, the doorbell rang, and I opened the door to find a man standing there. "Uh . . . is your mother home?" he stammered. I was a child, but I understood why he was there. I shifted my gaze downward to the floor. "No, she isn't home." I recognized the man from the church choir. I felt so ashamed and dirty, even though it had nothing to do with me. I knew he was married and had children because one of his children sang in the choir with me.

My mother also carried on an affair for many years with her married boss. Observing my mother's behavior was devastating to me. I internalized a great deal of shame as a result of her actions. It's no wonder I became disenchanted with marriage.

I did like her boss at first, though. He seemed to be a kind, fatherly sort, and we spent time with his wife and family. It was bizarre, of course, considering the affair. I never knew if his wife suspected anything, but she treated me kindly.

They had a barn with horses, and when I was a teenager, the family allowed me to ride whenever I wanted. It was a dream come true! My spirit soared as I rode through the fields. No matter what weighed heavily on my heart, a gallop through the forest and fields made everything right with my world.

When I was around eighteen years old, I was tacking up the horse in the barn one day to go for a ride when my mother's boss squeezed into the stall with me.

"That's a nice halter top," he said, gently placing his hand on my back. "Did you make it?"

"Yes," I replied, my face flushing red, bile rising in my throat.

"Would you like me to take it off?"

"No!" I managed to squeak out, quickly gathering the horse's reins and rushing out of the stall.

Fortunately, he never made another advance toward me, and I didn't mention it to my mother for quite some time. I understood that my mother justified her actions because she unconsciously adopted a victim mentality. In her mind, none of the rage and hysteria fueled by alcohol that she had subjected my brother and me to was her fault.

"Your goddamn father and that black-haired bitch he married! How could that son of a bitch leave us so destitute?" On and on, she would rage. When I was younger, I hid in my room to escape her tirades.

After I moved back in with her to care for Jamie, I read an article about "victim mentality" and decided I would not live like my mother. No matter what, I would take responsibility for my life and my choices. The article described victim mentality as a psychological concept referring to a mindset where a person tends to see themselves as a victim of others' negative actions. It's rooted in trauma, distress, and pain, creating feelings of anger or helplessness. In my case, it stemmed from years of my mother's rage and self-destructive behavior that affected my brother and me. I observed her unwillingness to confront or work through any part of her marriage's dissolution. At that stage in her life, my mother never considered that there was another way to deal with this trauma beyond drinking. To avoid repeating this behavior with my own child, I knew I needed to reorient myself toward my life decisions. Sometimes, as a parent, I'm sure my children have learned as much about what not to do as they have about what they should do!

As I became willing to take responsibility, it helped me finally move away from Alex without becoming consumed by anger. In fact, I rarely asked him for anything. Certainly, the thought of holding him accountable for bringing a child into this world never occurred to me! (I may have taken my newfound accountability a little too far; I only needed to explore my part and accept responsibility for my actions—not take on everyone else's.)

When I was free from Alex, a part of me truly enjoyed it, and I gradually started to build a life for myself. While my mother babysat Jamie, I went out with my childhood friend Patti, who had just separated from her husband.

"Let's go to the Ale House for a drink!" she said.

"Just walk into a bar by ourselves?" I asked.

"Yes, it'll be fun! You probably know some people there."

Alex and I never went to bars. Our social life revolved mostly around members of the devotional community, who also didn't frequent bars. So, I found myself staring at the front door of the Ale House, unable to enter.

"Go in!" Patti said. "What are you waiting for?"

"Are you sure about this?" Even at twenty-five years old, I felt strange about going to a bar.

"Yes!" Patti exclaimed, shoving me through the door.

I stumbled into the bar, and sure enough, I immediately saw a group of people I knew well—a large circle of friends from high school. I had a beer and caught up on the latest "goings-on." I felt . . . *normal.*

During the evening, a man approached me—someone I ran into from time to time. I had seen him sitting at the bar with his date, and when a seat opened up beside me, he took it and said hello. His date didn't look happy, but I had consumed enough drinks by then that I didn't really care.

"So, I heard you're not with Alex anymore," he said.

"Yes, that's true."

"Maybe we could go out sometime?"

"Sure, Angelo, that would be great."

I had always liked Angelo. He was older and had graduated from high school before me, but he was very charming, good-looking, and had no shortage of girlfriends. Angelo was, to me, the polar opposite of Alex. He worked out at the gym, was an athlete, and was very attractive. He had a wonderful smile and laugh. We had known each other through friends for quite some time, and I always felt a connection with him. When I started working with psychics, I discovered that we had many lifetimes together, as mother and son, as lovers; some lifetimes were violent. I had a lot of "history" with this soul.

When we began dating, our relationship was very tumultuous. We were on again, off again with a great deal of fighting. He was jealous and possessive. Occasionally, after being at the bars with his friends, he would come over and knock on my window.

As a single mom working full-time at that point, I didn't go out much. However, I had fallen deeply in love with Angelo and welcomed him into my bed each time. He climbed in with me and held me tightly. I could feel how much he loved me, yet he seemed hesitant to acknowledge the depth of his feelings. I never spoke of our love either. Perhaps I was afraid that if I said something, it would disappear.

When Jamie was three, Angelo came over one evening and wanted to make love. I told him that I had to have my IUD out for ten days because of a medical problem, so it wasn't safe to have sex. "Don't worry. Trust me—it will be fine," he reassured me.

I felt uncomfortable, and, of course, he did *not* pull out before he came. In fact, he was inside me for less than a minute. I felt angry and betrayed by his disrespect toward me. I had always taken great care with contraception after Jamie was born. Still, it had taken Alex and me nearly a year to conceive Jamie, so I figured I would be okay.

You guessed it! I immediately missed a period, started to feel nauseated, and knew right away that I was pregnant. I also understood that under *no* circumstances would I bring another child into this world. I simply saw no other option, so I began to make arrangements for an abortion. I told Angelo that I was pregnant and intended to terminate the pregnancy. It didn't seem to faze him much. At least, if it did, he didn't let on.

Shortly before the abortion, a friend stopped by to see how I was doing. The two of us used to drive together to the ashram in Philadelphia at least once a week to listen to holy discourse. She looked down at me as I lay on the couch, exhausted and nauseated, and said, "I came over to give you a message."

She abruptly sat down beside me and closed her eyes. When she opened them, her gaze was so filled with love that a beautiful, soft light radiated from her being as she began to speak.

"You are loved." She paused to look closely at me. "What you're doing isn't wrong. It's okay. There is no mistake in your decision to have an abortion. You're not alone. We are here for you, and you are loved."

At that moment, I felt enveloped in a soft cloud of what seemed to me like divine love. A flood of tears, coupled with a lump in my throat the size of a tennis ball, rendered me speechless.

My friend briefly closed her eyes, reopened them, and looked at me with a puzzled expression. "I don't know what just happened," she said.

"I felt as if Jesus were speaking through you," I told her.

At that time, neither of us knew anything about channeling Spirit. I could sense that she felt somewhat embarrassed.

"That has only happened to me once before," she said. "I went to visit a friend who was very ill and felt something wash over me, and Jesus spoke to her as well."

We both found it strange that, in both instances, she believed it was Jesus rather than our guru. Her visiting my apartment at that time of day was out of character, but I was profoundly moved by the message and the comfort I received. So, I cherished it, and tucked it away in my heart.

The day I went to the hospital for the abortion, Angelo's sister looked after Jamie for me. I never told anyone in my family because I was too ashamed. Though distressed, I held onto the belief in my heart that I was doing the right thing.

I will always be grateful to Planned Parenthood. I was able to plan for a safe, low-cost abortion. (Angelo split the cost with me.) Nonetheless, the decision to terminate a live fetus developing inside my uterus caused me profound anguish.

In the recovery room, I opened my eyes to see a young doctor sitting next to my bed. When he noticed my eyes were open, he took hold of my hand. "We have many young girls who come to our clinic sometimes two or three different times to get an abortion. It means nothing to them. It seems to be their form of birth control. However, I could see you were deeply distressed by your condition, so I wanted to be here when you woke up to offer you comfort."

"Was it a boy or a girl?" was all I could manage to ask.

"We don't share that type of information," he replied.

"Oh . . . okay."

I found it unusual for a doctor in such a busy clinic to take the time to sit with me, but I was glad he did.

"You're going to be fine," he said, smiling at me. Then, he withdrew his hand and left.

There it was again, that brief moment of Divine Grace appearing, when I felt so ashamed and unworthy. This episode, along with others, was a portent of God's love that I would gradually come to embrace with great humility and gratitude.

After the abortion, I continued my relationship with Angelo, which, of course, remained tumultuous. He insisted on living by an infuriating double standard: he could date or sleep with whomever he wanted, but I was expected to remain his exclusive girlfriend. It *never* occurred to me that I deserved a healthier relationship or that I should be treated well, or even how to recognize such a situation.

My mother, father, and stepmother did absolutely nothing to model any aspect of what a healthy relationship might look like. I was pulled into Angelo's orbit in a gravitational field of dysfunction I was nowhere near able to see, understand, or manage at that time. I was a people pleaser because I could not stand creating any discord, no matter how harmful it might be to myself. I now realize that part of this "gravitational pull" was also past life issues playing out.

One night, Angelo showed up late as he had been told by a mutual friend that I was seeing another man. He burst into my apartment, ignoring my mother's pleas, and came straight for me. I didn't cower. I stood tall, filled with so much rage and anger that this two-timing, double-standard jerk would dare confront me.

"Get the hell out of my apartment and *out of my life!*" I bellowed directly in his face.

He continued yelling at me for a moment—but then left.

That behavior clinched the deal. I was finally finished with Angelo. I didn't want to put my mother, my young son, or myself through anything like that again!

Then the flowers began to arrive, followed by the begging and the promises of "I will never do that again." He would also call me at work, putting on a full-court press for redemption.

Once again, I weakened and took him at his word. I loved him, and surely he would *never* do that again. I agreed to resume our relationship but told him that if he wanted me to be faithful to him, he also had to be faithful to me. And so it was that we dated exclusively after that episode.

When Jamie was seven, the other half of the double house next to Angelo's mother's residence became available for rent. Angelo wanted me to move in.

"No," I said, "not unless you want to get married."

"Okay, then, let's do it," he said.

I believed it was an opportunity for Jamie to finally have a proper, normal family. I pushed all concerns out of my mind. Denial is a potent drug!

I loved Angelo; however, we had a very rocky and difficult dating relationship fraught with arguments and disappointments. I broke up with him several times, and he always convinced me to come back, making promises that things would get better. I was in denial. It was an all-encompassing refusal to believe or accept the truth. I wasn't clear enough in understanding or listening to my intuition; plagued with self-doubt and confusion, I entered my marriage from that place of denial. But God granted me grace through the consequences of my actions.

Angelo came from a large, gregarious extended family of Italian immigrants, and I loved his mother. I knew my mother had her doubts about my move, but she never expressed them.

Meanwhile, my father and stepmother were over the moon that I was finally getting married. My father hadn't met Jamie until he was five years old, when a business trip brought him to Philadelphia. I guess he had softened enough that he finally wanted to meet his grandson; I suspect he never mentioned this to my stepmother. During his visit, while having dinner with him, my father defended his judgment of my life choices, including Jamie's birth. I understood why my choices looked bizarre and irresponsible to him. I judged myself for them, too. But I stopped him mid-sentence, looked him right in the eye, and took a deep breath. "How dare you judge me! Do you know what my life was like after you left? Do you realize the hell you put us through? How I suffered at the hands of you, Mom, and your current wife?"

I had never spoken to my father in that way, but I continued. "I've had enough of your criticism! Take a look at what your actions did to us before you look down on me!" My father's eyes started to fill with tears. *Oh my God!* I thought. *He actually heard me!*

"You're right," he said, looking down at his plate. "I have no right to judge you. I'm sorry. I never considered how the divorce affected you." That conversation would never have happened if Patricia had been present. This was between my father and me.

I have always shared a profound, unbreakable connection with my father and brother. A deep love exists between us that seems to transcend our human flaws—an invisible force that inexplicably binds the three of us. Perhaps Patricia sensed this unconsciously, triggering her reaction.

My father and I moved on to discuss other topics quickly, as there was no need to belabor the point.

Things shifted a bit after that. I moved in with Angelo and prepared for my wedding, and I actually grew quite close to my stepmother, Patricia. I spoke with her often and sought her advice about work and life. She liked Angelo. When we drove to West Virginia to visit, she and my father took Angelo to the country club to play golf and share some laughs. I felt accepted and "legitimate."

She even flew in from West Virginia to help me decorate our little home. She made a complete set of curtains for the house, bought us a couch as a wedding gift, and assisted me in choosing my wedding dress. I knew my father was ecstatic that Patricia and I were getting along so well, but the robustness of our relationship was predicated on my agreeing with her as she criticized my brother and sister-in-law. They had apparently done or said something to set her off. It never felt right to me, as I loved my brother and his wife dearly. I had not yet learned how to deal with such a situation authentically.

Angelo and I were to be married in the Catholic Church. The day before the wedding, I met with one of the priests to complete some paperwork, as I had been unable to find my baptismal certificate. I later discovered that I never had one. The priest said, "Well, then, I'm going to have to list you as agnostic."

Having spent many years in the Episcopalian Church as a member of the youth choir, I took objection to that. I certainly did believe in God and Christ. (However, I chose not to mention my foray into the Hindu religion.)

"Father, I am *not* an agnostic. If you insist on labeling me as such, I will refuse to marry in your church!"

He looked down with a sigh and said, "Oh . . . well, okay." I'm not sure what he wrote on that form, but we began planning the marriage ceremony without delay.

On the day of the wedding, my mother, brother, sister-in-law, their young daughter, my father, and Patricia all made their way to the church (in separate cars, of course). During a particular part of the ceremony, Angelo and I were to sit in chairs opposite each other, about eight feet apart, as the priest spoke of the sanctity of marriage. I closed my eyes for a moment while he spoke. My soul spoke to me. "This is a mistake. You should not marry this man, and you know it!"

God help me, I knew it was true. Great timing.

I ignored the message from my soul and went through with the marriage anyway. What else could I do? Every time I tried to break up with Angelo, he pursued me with fierce intensity, always convincing me to come back. I kept thinking it would "get better." In the back of my mind, I think I was afraid of him. *I'm doing this for Jamie*, I told myself.

Not surprisingly, my marriage to Angelo was fraught with difficulties. I made the rookie mistake of believing I could change him, but he saw no reason to alter his ways. Of course, during the four and a half years we were married, we shared some wonderful moments. He adopted Jamie not long after our wedding, which I considered a noble act on his part. When we were in the judge's chambers finalizing the adoption, the judge looked directly at Angelo and remarked, "You realize, Angelo, that you are now Jamie's father by law, and should you ever get divorced, you will be held responsible for Jamie's financial support."

Adoption meant that Jamie's birth certificate was updated to reflect Angelo as his father. I suppose the judge realized that even though it was a joyful occasion, he better cover all bases. It was yet another moment when my inner voice stirred, albeit quietly.

Deeply ingrained in my psyche was my expectation of marriage. I loved Angelo; he loved me. If we prioritized addressing any marital issues that arose, we could strengthen and grow our marriage. Although we had not done anything of the sort during our four years of dating, I believed that once we were married, that would change.

I was again so focused on taking responsibility for making my marriage work that I couldn't embrace the WE that was necessary. In truth, Angelo saw absolutely no reason to change anything, period. While my ideals were noble, I eventually felt that my soul was dying. Our lack of compatibility in so many areas of our marriage took a toll on my psyche and my health. We truly had separate lives. I took vacations on my own or with Jamie and socialized with my own group of friends, especially within the devotional community. We even had separate bank accounts.

I attempted a separation for three months one summer, during which Jamie and I stayed with my mother. The discord in our marriage significantly heightened Jamie's challenges, and

I grew increasingly concerned. When we returned, Angelo assured me that he would put more effort into our marriage. "Things will get better," he promised me again.

Entering this marriage from a place of denial made it impossible to experience it as I had envisioned. Denial created an imbalance in my desire to change after our marriage and Jamie's adoption. Simply put, I could not fix something that was broken without understanding how and why it was broken, and I could not fix it alone.

No amount of meditation would work if I hadn't learned how to "listen." When I was finally able to confront the collateral damage my denial had caused, I was in a great deal of pain. As I look at this now, it reminds me of wading into the ocean and standing just where the waves are breaking on me, knocking me all to hell and gone. I realize that I need to go farther into the ocean, and my experience becomes much more pleasant.

The gift of being uncomfortable was the catalyst for change.

CHAPTER 6

Joining Shirley Out on a Limb

"There are more things in heaven and
earth, Horatio, than are dreamt of in
your philosophy."

—*WILLIAM SHAKESPEARE,* HAMLET

In April 1986, I flew to Florida to visit a friend. One day, while
she was at work, I sat on her floor, staring at her bookshelf for
something to read. My finger ran along the middle row of her
bookcase and came to rest on a paperback edition of *Out on a
Limb* by Shirley MacLaine. With the book in hand, I headed
to the beach.

I became completely immersed in the book. She spoke
of psychic readings, crystals, extraterrestrials, past lives, and
healers who could perform amazing feats. Everything Shirley described in her book resonated deeply with my soul. It
was a whole new level of spiritual learning, and I wanted to
experience all of it! I wanted to "find" my crystal, get a psychic
reading, visit a healer, and go to the Bodhi Tree bookstore on
Melrose Avenue in Los Angeles. I longed to explore the places
she discussed—Machu Picchu in Peru; Sedona, Arizona; and

73

Santa Fe, New Mexico. (I was less enthusiastic about meeting extraterrestrials.)

Shirley's book had a tremendous impact on me. Even though many of her Hollywood peers labeled her as a nutcase, what she wrote resonated deeply within my heart and soul. I returned to Angelo rejuvenated by this new knowledge and the world I had discovered in Shirley's book.

That summer, Jamie, my mother, and I traveled to Northern California for three weeks to visit my brother and his family. Jamie and I also took a break and flew down to Los Angeles to spend time with my friend Angela.

"Angela, do you know of a bookstore called the Bodhi Tree?" I asked her.

"Yeah, it's a new age bookstore on Melrose. I know where it is."

"Great!" I exclaimed excitedly. "Can we go there?"

"Sure, we can check it out, I suppose."

The next morning, Angela, Jamie, and I jumped into her Volkswagen Beetle and headed to the Bodhi Tree. I was beside myself with joy. New age books, crystals, and who knew what else awaited me. As I roamed around the store, exploring the different sections, a few books unexpectedly fell off the shelf onto my pile! I was in complete bliss.

Meanwhile, Angela had plopped down in a chair, wearing a disgruntled expression of boredom.

"Why are you so into this? We have been on a spiritual journey with our guru for years, and we've done everything possible to evolve our consciousness!"

"No, no, no! There's so much more! This stuff is really amazing," I blurted out as I darted into another room.

Jamie was knee-deep in the tarot card section. He had always possessed the ability to "see" earthbound spirits, so the Bodhi Tree held great promise to satiate his curiosity.

At the checkout counter, there was a glass-topped case filled with crystals. "Ah! Here they are," I exclaimed. "I wonder how I'll know which one is *my* crystal?"

I stared at them, touched a few, and waited for a sign. Then, almost as an afterthought, Angela, who was now standing next to me, reached out to touch a beautiful, large crystal lying on the tray.

"Wendy," she said, "my frigging hand and forearm are heating up!" Her eyes were wide as she lifted her hand off the crystal so I could touch her and feel the heat.

When I felt the warmth of her hand and forearm, I exclaimed, "Holy shit!" Her arm was also vibrating gently.

"My God, this must be *your* crystal," I said with some dismay. "Great! I fly three thousand miles to come to this bookstore to find *my* crystal, and you, completely uninterested, find *yours*."

Unfortunately, I had to acknowledge that I didn't connect with any of the crystals for sale at the Bodhi Tree that day, but I did have my book selections.

"I can't afford two hundred dollars for this crystal!" Angela moaned. "I don't know what to do. Maybe I should come back another time."

"Look, you have to buy this crystal. It's for you!" I said. I knew she lived on a tight budget and was trying to make ends meet, so her protest was valid. "Listen, if this is meant for you, the money will come. Just trust and buy it." I quietly hoped that what I had read about higher good and abundance was indeed true.

Angela stared at me, then at the crystal for a moment. I could tell she sensed something mystical was happening.

When we returned to her apartment with her crystal in tow, she paused to check her mail. To her surprise, she found a card from her grandmother, even though her birthday had already passed. Inside the card was a check for $200! We exchanged glances, and I was equally stunned by the timing. Wow, we were seriously on to something!

"Let me see those damn books you just bought," Angela said. She continued to make numerous forays back to the Bodhi Tree after that experience.

Months later, I was at my job filling out an accident report for a woman who had twisted her ankle on the tennis court. Her name stood out to me, though I didn't know why.

At that moment, Angela called me. "Oh my God! I just got off the phone with a psychic!"

"Wow, how did you find a psychic?"

"A friend of mine mentioned a reading she had with this woman in Sedona, and she was completely blown away! So, I asked for the woman's name and number."

Since I had known Angela for many years, it was easy for me to see just how accurate the psychic's reading had been. After hearing that, I had to get a reading, too. When Angela gave me the psychic's name, I realized that her last name was the same as the woman who had twisted her ankle. Uncanny!

It made sense to me that someone could possess psychic abilities. Ever since I was a young girl, I had been able to sense or feel things before they happened. I knew as I grew older that I had what we then called extrasensory perception, or ESP. However, I blocked it out because it made me feel different and strange.

Before my marriage to Angelo, I would take Jamie and me to a naturopathic doctor who was recommended to me by the devotional community. Those types of doctors weren't abundant in the 1970s. Toward the end of my appointment, I asked her a question.

"Doctor Carrie, are you familiar with ESP?"

She paused her writing, stood up from her desk, and sat beside me on the exam table. "Yes, I know quite a bit about it. I've nurtured it within myself to enhance my practice."

"I used to have episodes of knowing things before they happened," I told Carrie. "But it scared the hell out of me. I don't want to be able to see that someone is going to die! It's a horrible burden to carry." (Clearly, I had seen too many episodes of *The Twilight Zone*.)

"Wendy," Carrie said, "it's not a random experience. It's God. You'll only receive information when it's for the highest good of either the person or yourself. Practice asking what you should do with the information, and what action you need to take for the highest good of everyone involved."

The information she shared with me was incredibly cathartic. I wasn't a crazy person after all! It wasn't long before I would be put to the test. Shortly after my doctor's appointment, I began to feel that familiar sensation while visiting my mother.

This sensation included clammy hands and nausea. My mother had a bad cold and wasn't feeling well, but she insisted it was "nothing a few days off from work wouldn't cure."

I was cognizant of the fact that my mother still drank and smoked heavily, which put her at risk for a heart attack at the very least. Before I left for home, I went next door to talk to her neighbor Dottie, who was a dear friend.

"Dottie, you might find this is weird, but I need your help."

"No problem, sweetie. What can I do for you?"

"Well, I have a strong feeling something is wrong with my mother beyond a cold. Would you promise me, if you notice anything—even the slightest deviation from her routine—that you will call me no matter what time of day? I worry that she's going to have a stroke or heart attack very soon."

Dottie and I had discussed psychic abilities before, and I knew she believed in them and understood precisely what I was asking of her. She promised she would call me.

The next morning, while I was opening my office and getting my coffee, Dottie called.

"Wendy, dear, you asked me to call you if anything unusual happened, no matter how minor. I feel silly bothering you, but I promised. Your mother came over for coffee this morning and asked me why I had been in her room last night. Now, you know I wasn't in her room, but she insisted she saw me there. I told her she must have been dreaming, but she said it felt so real."

My internal alarm bell blasted. I thanked Dottie and quickly called my mother's doctor. "I think my mother is having a heart attack or a stroke," I informed him.

"What are her symptoms?" he asked.

Oh shit, I thought. *I can't tell him I'm having a psychic episode.*

"Uh . . ." I stammered. "She's . . . uh . . . *confused.*"

"Hmmm . . ." the doctor said. "Well, I can see her in a few days. Why don't you make an appointment and bring her in?"

"No, I'm taking her to the emergency room. I will see you there." I realized this was brazen, as I had given the doctor very little to go on from a medical perspective. I hesitated for a moment after getting off the phone with her doctor, suddenly feeling unsure of myself.

"It's now or never," I said sternly to myself.

I then rushed to my mother's apartment. She was sitting up in bed, reading. She looked at me over the top of her reading glasses and said, "Oh, hi, honey. What are you doing here?"

"Mother, get dressed. I'm taking you to the hospital *now!*" I said firmly.

"For God's sake, Wendy, don't be ridiculous. I just have a cold. What's gotten into you?"

"Mother," I said, setting my teeth, "either you get up and get dressed right now or I'm calling an ambulance. What's it going to be?"

"Jesus Christ, you have gone off your rocker!" she said.

"Maybe, but I can live with that. Either way, we're going to the hospital now."

My panic rose as I noticed my mother's speech was slightly slurred.

When we arrived at the emergency room, my mother unleashed a litany of curse words, punctuated by her insistence that the cough medicine was responsible for her disorientation. As reasonable as that might have sounded, I wasn't buying it.

"What's the problem, miss?" the nurse asked, looking back and forth between my mother and me, unsure which one of us was the patient.

"My daughter thinks I'm having a stroke or heart attack," my mother said. "I really just have a cold. She's overreacting."

The nurse glanced at me impatiently.

"Listen," I said, "my mother is slurring her words and is disoriented." I was becoming exasperated. "You need to tend to her immediately!" I figured, in the worst-case scenario, I would appear to be a daughter who was a nutcase.

Fortunately, they placed her in a room and connected her to a heart monitor as I proceeded to complete the paperwork for her admission. By the time I finished, a flurry of activity surrounded my mother's cubicle. They were hooking her up to IVs and additional monitors. She was indeed in serious trouble. I entered the waiting room, and her doctor walked in and looked at me. "What were your mother's symptoms again?" Feeling exhausted, I took a deep breath and said, "Don't worry about it. It's not in your medical books. Just tell me what's happening."

My mother had severe hypertension and had developed an enlarged heart, which, in turn, was sending blood clots through her arteries; one of the clots had likely lodged in her brain. This was what caused her to think she saw her neighbor in her room. It explained why I sensed both a heart attack and a stroke. In a way, it truly was both!

In later conversations with my mother, she admitted to experiencing additional symptoms. She continually heard music despite the radio being off. Out of fear, she masked her feelings, as was her usual approach.

By embracing my psychic abilities as a gift rather than a curse, I was able to save my mother's life that day and cherish twenty more years with her!

Later in the year, on Christmas Day, Angelo and I visited her. Dottie and her husband walked over from next door to say hello. Dottie was in her sixties and quite a character. She always wore an outrageous wig, her long fingernails were painted with cheap red polish, and her eyebrows were drawn with dark black pencil. The greatest thing about Dottie, though, was her checkered past, both good and bad. Dottie's husband, Rusty, was a gentle and kind man (especially since he no longer drank) of Irish and Native American descent. His walk was stiff and slow due to Parkinson's disease. I loved them both dearly. I hugged Dottie and wished her a Merry Christmas. She pulled back slightly, saying her shoulders were very sore, and we shared a chuckle about old age. Then, she sat down on the couch next to me, reached out, and grabbed my hand as we continued our visit. After they went home, Rusty returned within fifteen minutes, banging on my mother's door.

"Help! Something happened to Dottie! She just slumped over while we were watching TV!" Rusty was usually a quiet man, but suddenly, he was so hysterical that he couldn't even call the paramedics. I was trained in CPR, so I instructed my mother to call an ambulance while I started CPR on Dottie.

Rusty wanted to lay Dottie out on the couch with a pillow under her head and a soft blanket covering her, but I quickly explained that a hard surface was necessary for performing chest compressions. So, we moved her to the floor. I was shaking because I had never had to use my CPR training on anything other than the rubber dummies provided by the Red Cross. But I worked on Dottie until the paramedics arrived and got set up.

I knew her lungs were filled with fluid, but I continued, even though the fluid had begun to leak from the side of her mouth. When the paramedics took over, they congratulated me for keeping her oxygenated, as her color remained healthy.

I got up and stood back as they worked feverishly on her. I felt her spirit lift out of her body and stand on the other side of the living room. Normally, their cocker spaniel barked furiously, trying to bite any strangers who came in, but he sat quietly by the spot where I felt Dottie's spirit was standing.

When Dottie and I had spent time together earlier in the evening, I didn't sense, psychically, that she was in danger. Tragically, she passed away within an hour from a massive heart attack. Carrie had been correct. I would experience psychic episodes only when there was something I needed to know or act on.

When I made my phone appointment with Jan, the psychic, she immediately stated that my guides were present and eager to begin. "You are very miserable in your current marriage. You need to stop deceiving yourself and examine this situation. The man you are married to is not going to evolve himself or this marriage as you have hoped. It's crushing your soul and could make you very ill." Well, she certainly didn't mince words!

As she spoke, tears streamed down my face. The lump in my throat made it so all I could do was listen as I was told what I hadn't been able to admit to myself. I knew, however, that her words were irrefutably true. I had desperately tried to find a way to make my marriage work, believing I was nobly taking responsibility for my choices.

Jan, however, informed me that Angelo and I had shared many lifetimes together and that we had a significant amount of "history" from our various incarnations on Earth. The notion of having lived other lives was not unfamiliar to me, as it is a fundamental aspect of Hinduism. However, I had not personally explored past life issues manifesting in my current existence.

Jan proceeded to explain the lifetimes relevant to my marriage with Angelo. In particular, she referred to my abortion, which I had not disclosed to her at all. In one lifetime, she stated, Angelo belonged to a marauding band of men attacking the castle where I resided. He raped and impregnated me. Despite being assaulted by an enemy invader, I was still treated poorly and lived with shame.

As Jan spoke, I started to grasp the deeper meaning of the events surrounding my abortion, why my angelic guides had sent my friend to channel Jesus, and why, when I awoke after the procedure, the doctor was holding my hand.

"Your guides knew you understood the sacredness of life," Jan continued. "By aborting this child, you were creating a balance of past life patterns between you and Angelo. The tender care of your spirit confused you because you didn't feel worthy of such care. This confusion arose because you didn't understand soul agreements."

Exploring my history with Angelo this way helped me better understand the challenges in our relationship, laying the groundwork for forgiveness for both myself and Angelo. Receiving this new understanding from Jan did not lessen the emotional trauma, however. I still felt the same emotionally, but I began to gain a broader perspective that, over time, would allow me to achieve a more balanced emotional response.

"Jan," I said, "I know I have to leave this marriage, but I'm afraid of his temper. I don't want him to come to my workplace and cause trouble for me. He has always managed to convince me to come back. When he realizes that I'm truly not returning, he'll show up at my job or my mother's house. He won't give up." I wasn't genuinely worried for my physical safety, but I was concerned about emotional harassment.

Jan shared with me how to connect with Angelo's higher self and how to ask for what I needed as I left the marriage. Late at night, I would communicate with Angelo's higher self, always expressing gratitude and love as fully as I could—not just to Angelo, but to his immediate family as well. Jan explained that higher-self work is very sacred and powerful, and it is only effective in specific circumstances.

This speaks to the concept of one of the guiding principles I follow: the understanding that we are not physical bodies possessing a soul; rather, we are souls inhabiting a physical body. We never fully separate from Source as we incarnate, but we experience our physical bodies. So, when I prayed and spoke to Angelo's higher self, the soul connected to Source, I was addressing that part of his being.

One morning, after working with the process through the night, I awoke to find Angelo sobbing next to me. He knelt on the floor, begging me not to leave him. I had not yet attempted to discuss my plans to end our marriage and move out. I didn't say a word; I just squeezed my eyes tightly shut.

He'll be devastated and heartbroken when I leave, I thought. *He treats me so thoughtlessly and poorly, though. Despite my pleas and warnings, he doesn't seem capable of change. God, please help us both.*

That May, while Angelo's parents, who lived in the other half of the house, were away, I borrowed a friend's van and took the day off while Angelo was at work. I moved our dog, my clothes, Jamie's clothes, and some other belongings out of our house. I tried to leave the place looking as if nothing were missing. As I put the van in Reverse and pulled out of the driveway for the last time, I felt a great weight lift off my shoulders. No one bothered me during my exodus. It was truly a miracle.

Jamie and I moved back in with my mother. Jamie mentioned that Grannie's apartment had always felt like "home" to him, and he felt safe there. After settling in, I felt relieved yet unsettled. I sensed a significant shift in my psyche, but I had no idea what was going to happen next.

My expectations of marriage and creating a happy family with the three of us were completely shattered. I had failed, and it hurt like hell.

CHAPTER 7

Harmonic Convergence

"If we do not change our direction, we
are likely to end up where we are headed."

—ANCIENT CHINESE PROVERB

I continued to work with Jan to guide me through that period
of significant change and expansion. It was exhilarating yet
painfully slow. I wanted my soulmate and my wonderful new
life to begin immediately! *I longed for the pain of my shattered
life to dissipate.* I was at the initial stage—the low end—of a
powerful new learning curve, becoming aware of forces I hadn't
recognized before. I sensed great opportunities awaiting me. I
was free, with nothing holding me back. Well, nothing except
the outdated belief systems that no longer supported who I
wanted to become, of course, which became increasingly evident as I worked with Jan.

By my "self," I refer to aspects of my being—my ego,
personality, and learned belief systems. The pathway to alignment and balance was laid out for me to examine and feel.
A new level of understanding was blooming in my consciousness, building upon "taking complete responsibility" for my
life. A seed of understanding germinated; my life could be a

87

co-creative process in that I would do the necessary work on myself in partnership with God. Guru Maharaji had shown me that God is within, and that a true consciousness of bliss is indeed attainable. Meditation, doing service for the community (devotional), and listening to holy discourse were genuine pathways, but I wanted to explore my gift of intuition and my curiosity about different spiritual topics.

I had the opportunity to meet Jan in person in August 1987 and participate in a live reading. I took some vacation time while Jamie attended an overnight camp to fly to Sedona for the "Harmonic Convergence." The event comprised the world's first globally synchronized meditation that occurred on August 16–17, 1987, coinciding with an alignment of planets in the solar system. The timing of the Harmonic Convergence was also significant according to the Mayan calendar, as well as European and Asian astrological traditions, and the dates of the Convergence marked the planetary alignment of the sun, moon, and six other planets.

Angela also flew in for the Harmonic Convergence, and she took me to a party one evening. I stood on the porch, staring up at the night sky, which was brilliantly lit with what appeared to be millions of stars. A warm breeze carried the scents of the summer desert. I was awestruck by the sight. Then, I noticed that some of the "stars" seemed to be moving—slowly, quickly, then darting off suddenly, at a right angle.

Angela stepped out onto the porch with me, and she also looked up. Then, we exchanged glances. "Oh my God!" I exclaimed. "Look at that! It looks like some intergalactic airport!"

Indeed, it appeared that there was a great deal of UFO-like

objects coming and going. I had never witnessed anything like it.

Angela turned to me and quipped, "Ha ha! We're not in Kansas anymore, Toto. Welcome to Sedona!"

When I finally tore myself away from the spectacle in the sky, I returned inside to discover a group of people attentively listening to a woman who was "channeling."

Channeling spirit differs from the psychic readings I had with Jan. The woman explained that her consciousness would begin to expand, open, and deepen. Then, a spiritual being would speak *through* her. Some channelers speak with their eyes closed, while others keep their eyes open. She was not aware of what was being said because her conscious awareness was "parked" elsewhere. Her personality did not filter the information, making it feel like speaking directly with great spirits, free from ego or personality interruptions.

Her body and mannerisms transformed, as did the clarity of her voice. The shift in the room's energy was palpable as the spiritual entity manifested. It felt powerful and benevolent, and the ensuing message overflowed with deep, ancient wisdom. I was profoundly moved.

At that time, people living on the West Coast were focused on the prediction of a major earthquake coinciding with the Harmonic Convergence. Someone in the group inquired about the "coming" earthquake. The channel adjusted slightly to face the individual asking the question and said, "Why would you want to direct your thoughts and energy toward that? Your collective thoughts hold great power. Pay attention, unless, of course, you actually wish for it to happen."

That was not the answer I expected! Spirit explained that earthquakes occur as they have for eons due to the shifting of the earth's tectonic plates, but our thoughts of fear, doom, and gloom introduce another dimension to the reality of earthquakes. Consider what we see every day on various platforms—be it the news, social media, or other communications. Focusing on that negativity only adds to the "spiral" of negativity. The adage "what you fear, you draw near" was ingrained in my psyche from that day forward. Overall, my first night in Sedona was truly an experience!

Sedona was filled with people celebrating the Convergence. I was struck by the diversity of the crowd. All races, ages, religions, and economic backgrounds were represented. It was a true cross section of humanity. This was unlike the peace gatherings I had experienced in the late '60s and early '70s, where we (hippies) all looked and dressed quite similarly. To me, it felt as if we had all been "invited" to the Convergence. There was a prevailing sense of deep calm and purpose.

I selected several organized events to attend. One particular event was a gathering of about twelve to work with teachers who would help us release past life patterns. After meditating, we boarded a van heading to a beautiful cottonwood grove by a stream. During the ride, I chatted with two of the facilitators and found them to be very loving, full of spirit and light.

"May I take your pictures?" I inquired after our arrival.

"Yes, you may," one of the women said. "You should know, however, that when you have the film developed, we will not appear in the picture."

"What? Why?"

"The souls inhabiting these bodies have granted us permission to allow our consciousness to reside within them in order to do this work with all of you. However, they wish to keep their identities anonymous, so we will raise our vibration, thus becoming invisible in the photo."

I should have been accustomed to that kind of thing by then, but I took the photo anyway. When I had the photos developed, there was no one in the picture, just as I had been told. All I had was a picture of the picnic table in the cottonwood grove.

I learned later that day that this type of "arrangement" is an agreement between a human being and another being not in human incarnation. They call themselves "walk-ins." A walk-in occurs when two souls agree to swap places. From my understanding, walk-ins are the result of an energetic process where the person has an agreement to allow another being who is not in physical incarnation to inhabit their body for a specific purpose of facilitating healing—or for teaching individuals or groups. It is similar to the process of channeling, however much more expanded, and, as always, aligned with the highest good. (Note: This is not to be confused with mental health conditions such as multiple personality disorder, now known as dissociative identity disorder.)

I had never encountered that term before that day, nor have I encountered it since.

I understand that some people believe channeling is the same as dissociative identity disorder. In my view, there is no basis for considering channeling a disorder. The individual who channels embraces the experience and does not experience blackouts when an alternate personality "takes over." The voice that emerges responds to questions from others in the room and communicates in a manner that offers counsel.

Our group gathered in the cottonwood grove for a meditation session to begin clearing blockages from past lives—or our current one. Afterward, as we got up to walk over to the river, I suddenly experienced excruciating pain in my lower back and lurched forward. The facilitators were immediately by my side.

"What's going on with you at this moment?" one of the women asked.

"I'm having a lot of pain in my lower back!" I exclaimed.

They immediately placed their hands on my lower back and guided me forward. A warm, prickly energy surged through my back, and the pain vanished instantly.

"Does that help?" they asked.

"Yes, wow! Thank you so much. The pain is completely gone!" I replied.

Of course, everything in the Universe is energy. It was clear to me that the experience I was having that day was an introduction to more advanced ways of using energy fields to create experiences for the highest good. The energy healing that coursed through my back was clearing a painful blockage I had been holding in my body from the exercises we were doing related to past lives. I don't know exactly the precise details of the issue that caused me pain with the blockage, but I knew that when they placed their hands on my lower back, the pain lifted immediately.

The rest of the afternoon, we played and swam in the stream. I felt blissful. Water has consistently transformed a great deal of spiritual, emotional, mental, and physical energy for me. Under the guidance of our facilitators, the experience was significantly enriched.

On the morning of the Harmonic Convergence celebration, everyone hiked up to specific "power spots" to meditate and pray. I hiked with Angela to one of the spots before sunrise. As I began to approach a group of people meditating, my intuition suddenly urged me to walk farther up the trail. I eventually reached a location with a magnificent view. There I stood alone, breathing in the sunrise as it started to crest the mountain range.

Sedona is known for its numerous "power vortices," believed to contain a great deal of energy. I realized that I was standing within the triangulation of a vortex called Bell Rock. (A vortex is a location, usually on or near an interesting rock formation, where people report feeling inspired by a beneficial source of energy.) As the sun crested the mountains, its rays shot out over the valley, bathing everything in warmth and light. In the center of the valley below, off in the distance from where I stood, was an iconic, giant monolithic rock formation often seen in photos of Sedona.

I stood transfixed and deeply humbled, feeling the great power of both seen and unseen things, known and unknown. I could sense the blessings, hope, and love that intensified through everyone's intentions as they came together to participate in the global, synchronized meditation throughout the day while the sunrise traveled across the globe. I have no words to express the gratitude and joy I felt that day.

I attended music concerts where harmonies and musical tones were played for us, unlike anything I had heard before. I can only describe them as "celestial." In contrast to the events in my life earlier that year, the weekend in Sedona felt like heaven on earth. It nourished my soul and curiosity beyond anything I could have imagined.

After returning home, Jan and I continued our phone readings, although she preferred to refer to her work as "psychic guidance." She would connect with my guides in writing and then mail the information to me.

During one particular reading, Jan said, "Wendy, I see three men entering your life. Each will teach you something different, but one of them appears to be your soulmate."

"Oh, great!" I exclaimed, laughing. "How Dickensian!"

Indeed, it was.

When I separated from Angelo, I knew I needed to reflect deeply on my previous relationships, in addition to my marriage, if I wanted to stop attracting this type of relationship. It was up to me to engage in this inventory with the understanding that it was about my growth. As Albert Einstein said, "You cannot solve a problem with the same consciousness that created it in the first place." I prayed for awareness, healing, and guidance.

I had recently met a man named Will through the devotional community, and we were deeply attracted to each other, sharing a strong connection. However, our relationship never really took off. He had a significant fear of pursuing a romantic involvement with me.

In one of her written readings, Jan discussed my connection with Will. These writings differed from our phone conversations; they were deeper and expressed differently. The following is an excerpt from her writing from January 1988:

"Do not be so dramatic in your healing process, because, Dear One, that suggests that life is about separation and that you are playing in the illusion. We have been with you many lifetimes, watching you navigate this illusion and getting confused by others' values. You have desired what you felt you needed then, not the needs that were buried deep within your being. You are very powerful and are here to serve your family; we do not mean an earthly family, but the family of your heavenly father. You chose this lifetime to stop playing in the illusion. Will is part of this process of healing. You have had many lifetimes where you did not live up to each other's expectations and desires, and you cannot do so in this lifetime either. This leads to intrigue and resentment—intrigue in continuing the challenge of molding one another and resentment when change does not occur. In this lifetime, these dynamics are played out very subtly. However, when you finally tire of meeting companions who cannot satisfy your inner thirst, you will surrender to the illusion of mates and turn inward to discover your true strength."

I had both an intellectual and spiritual understanding of the concepts of illusion and duality. The dictionary defines "illusion" as "a thing that is or is likely to be wrongly perceived or interpreted by the senses," and "duality" as "the state or quality of being two or in two parts."

Spiritually, I had the opportunity to experience my reality with a deeper and more expanded consciousness, guiding my choices in a more loving and mindful way. Spirit spoke to me repeatedly, just as the Mahatmas often shared in their discourse, about the need to rise "above" duality. Honestly, at the time, even though I knew their words were true, all I wanted was for Will to take me in his arms and make love to me passionately. Why couldn't we simply get past the impasse and love each other?

He called one day after I hadn't seen him for many weeks, asking if I wanted a ride to see our guru, who was giving a program in upstate New York. Surprised, I jumped at the chance to spend time with Will. As it turned out, I didn't see much of him during the program. I felt raw and uncertain, so I kept to myself most of the time, which is unusual for me since I usually socialized a great deal with my friends in the devotional community.

While driving home from the program, Will said, "I don't want to get involved with a woman who has a child with emotional issues."

I had shared with Will in earlier conversations that Jamie had been diagnosed as emotionally disturbed and placed in a special education class full-time at our local public school. The comment came out of the blue, and it was one of the cruelest things he could possibly have said to me. The words shocked and hurt me deeply. I don't remember responding; I just closed my eyes and rested my head back on the seat as if going to sleep.

Well, I thought, *congratulations, Will. That was quite effective. I fully understand that I need to let go and move on.*

Jamie had been through a lot, and I absolutely didn't want him to be exposed to any man who felt that way. In truth, Will's honesty, while painful, was a great blessing.

Soon after, Jan stayed with me for a week and offered psychic readings to my friends.

"Jan," I said to her one day, "I wonder what the evolutionary pathway of a soul looks like. Where does it lead? I understand the concept of past lives, the opportunity to learn lessons that bring more light, expansion, and healing to our beings. If we have the chance to evolve into angels or ascended masters, what happens next? Do we become angels and then stop? I'm pretty sure we can 'devolve'!"

We both sat quietly for a while, contemplating the possibilities.

"I believe we have opportunities to elevate our soul beings to God consciousness, allowing us to become the gods of our own universes," Jan mused.

"Yes, I can see that possibility myself, but even if our souls grew and expanded until we became gods of our own universes, would we still evolve, learn, and change?" I asked. "In fact, not to oversimplify, but a soul could then embark on a completely new learning curve!"

Oooh boy, I thought. *When I am cussing at God, I am, in truth, cursing at myself.*

Bearing in mind several factors, including the notion that the Universe is described as "infinite," it seemed that the possibilities for soul growth and expansion would also be infinite. Nothing in Creation is static. Albert Einstein stated, "Energy cannot be created or destroyed; it can only be changed from one form to another."

"Well, it stands to reason that the benevolent, all-knowing, loving being—God—whom we were always taught was perfect, may also be evolving. This renders the term 'perfect' a relative assignment, creating some true ramifications," I said.

"Yes, I believe so," Jan agreed.

I sat quietly, reflecting on my experience that day in New York City when I received my initiation through the Mahatma. It encompassed a vastness of consciousness and love, allowing me to feel as though I had experienced infinity and merged with God.

"I was taught from birth that God is perfect," I continued. "Yet, no one seems to truly understand what perfect is. It appears to me that this notion of perfection has only fostered judgment and confusion as humans pursue it, with an extreme example being Hitler attempting to create a 'master' race. Even Guru Maharaji was referred to as the 'Perfect Master' in the early days."

"Throughout history, there have been numerous interpretations of what perfection looks like. Many wars have been fought over whose religious figurehead was perfect or the 'one,'" Jan replied.

"So much killing occurs in the name of religious beliefs, perfection, and an all-loving, benevolent God. We should not see ourselves as separate from God. We are merely different parts of the human race expressing God in various ways."

"Yes, well, wouldn't that perception be a game changer?" Jan said.

The concept that God might continue to evolve was an epic paradigm shift for me. As I evolve, I embrace the axiom "When you know better, do better." I have learned, and endeavored to feel, react, or do something differently to reflect a higher understanding. Does this imply that the Creator also has the potential to change course and expand in new ways of understanding?

Not long after that visit with Jan, a friend from the devotional community stopped by. He brought a book he thought I would like, titled *Right Use of Will: Healing and Evolving the Emotional Body* by Ceanne DeRohan. This small paperback was published in Santa Fe. The information within was channeled through the author from Spirit. Much to my surprise, the book primarily discussed the origin of God consciousness, including the birth of God into consciousness ("In the beginning was the word . . .").

It also conveyed information about the creation of everything in our universe. It described the birth and evolution of God, along with the various types of spirits that were created. The book examined how, as God gained deeper understanding, changes were made to reflect that shift in awareness. The central theme for me was why we were endowed with free will and how that unfolded.

The author states: "The Will has for so long been judged against, controlled, disciplined, punished and denied that most of us no longer really know what our Will is. Many have been calling positive thinking by the mind Will power, but this is not really Will power so much as it is mind's power. While it is good to have a strong mind with all of its attributes and powers, when our mind is dominant, we are not giving full acceptance to the true essence of our Will. Our Will is the feminine aspect in all of us and expresses as emotion, intuition, receptivity and desire."

The author discussed how the darkness of the "void" and the brilliance of the "light" defined Creation. My newfound understanding of free will led me to believe that the Creator viewed it as the most loving gift that could be bestowed. I was free to evolve and experience, in all my bodies, the darkness and the light, reveling in my advancements, which were made all the more brilliant by my failures. I was, in fact, given free will to choose to align with the true nature of my will as part of my growth. The opportunity to realize, accept, and forgive all of myself across all my lifetimes—both good and bad—was not in opposition to God but rather in perfect alignment. I was grateful for the opportunity to consider the essence of my will, as I constantly seemed to be oriented toward pursuing *God's* will. I came to believe that we are not merely *in* God's image, but *are indeed* God's image.

In March of that year, I flew to Utah to ski and brought my new book along. One night during my stay, I awoke to the sensation of spirit guides standing at the right side of my bed. I wasn't afraid; in fact, I felt very safe, yet I kept my eyes closed. The guides sent a flow of golden liquid energy through my body, which felt heavenly as it cascaded from the top of my head down my arms. However, as the energy reached my solar plexus, I encountered a dark blockage, causing the energy flow to stop abruptly. It jolted me, and I suddenly felt sick and upset.

Oh, I have failed! I thought.

But before the thought could descend into self-loathing, I

heard the guides in my mind say, "No, no, no! Stop judging. We are simply trying to show you the state of your will. The density you feel is a result of stagnation and lack of light in your will. It's for you to bring into awareness but not to judge. Judging only creates more heaviness."

The author of *Right Use of Will* said, "Freedom of emotional expression is an important part of our Will's evolutionary path and can lead us to a greater depth of being. All of the emotions that have been labeled 'negative' are a part of what has been judged against and denied in our Will's expression." A prominent example of this is how often it has been said, "Do you choose love or fear?" Unconditional love would choose both by bringing our fears within love and finding out what they have to offer.

The book and the guides provided me with valuable teachings. Of course, this kind of awareness takes time to develop and integrate into everyday life. However, the concepts of an evolving God and aligning with my own divine will were significant additions to my growth and understanding.

Months passed before I felt the presence of my guides again. This time, they flanked me on either side of the bed, appearing as if in a dream, yet I was fully awake. It was not a dream, but rather a state outside of my physical body—what we often refer to as an "altered state." I observed a brown energy in a cross-hatched pattern undulating before me, and I sensed it contained a significant amount of fear.

"I don't like the way this feels," I said. "Why do I have to do this?"

My guides were silent and patient.

Suddenly, a man's face emerged in the center of the brown energy pattern.

"Who is that?" I asked. "I don't know that man!"

Once more, there was nothing but silence from my guides. This was starting to seriously agitate me, as I could not grasp the meaning or lesson at all. Yet, they revealed nothing to me.

The next morning, I woke up with a vivid recollection of the experience but still no clue about the identity of the man.

A few days later, while I was taking my run, I stopped and decided that maybe I should try something new. On my running route, there was a beautiful field to the right of the road. Although I felt foolish, I decided to step into this lovely field and try out this new exercise I had read about. I walked far enough away so that no one would hear me stating my declaration out loud. I self-consciously began, "God, I understand that it's my birthright to be happy and to ask for what I need because I'm worthy. Well, I need a place to live for Jamie and me!"

The introduction of what the Creator intended for me as my birthright was introduced to me in the book *Right Use of Will* in the early '80s, as I have mentioned. It resonated so deeply with me that it brought me to tears.

What I refer to as "my birthright" is a toolbox of gifts I am incarnated with. The frequency of Divine Source Energy, Creator, or God is a vibrational frequency of what I would call love. It is referred to as unconditional love because it holds no judgment. My soul was created from this frequency of vibration. One example I would use is grace. Even writing that word makes me want to cry at the depth of humility I experience, even when I am "crashing around in crazy town!" and suddenly something works out, help comes, and I gain awareness, seemingly out of nowhere. Well . . . it's grace. Another example I would use is that my prayers are *always* answered—always. Never in the way I think, but even better when I can move forward out of discomfort, because of trust.

The toolbox has a link to the Divine, and it is always there. I know I have had lifetimes where I was never aware of my toolbox, and I never accessed it. There is an infinite amount of gifts in my toolbox, and oh, what a joy it is as I discover how much I am loved and the delights that await me. This doesn't mean we will never experience pain, fear, or sorrow, but it does mean we can use the toolbox to gain a different perspective. It is the gift that enables us to move beyond being uncomfortable.

Somewhere in my unconsciousness, I believed that I was here to suffer and that I was a sinner. I knew God loved me; I had even experienced this benevolent love during my initiation. The idea that I incarnated with a set of items that were my birthright was so foreign, but I thought I would test out some of what that could mean on a practical level. I had read to ask with an open heart and to have no preconceived expectations of how this would manifest. It is my birthright to ask for help or for what I need; it's part of the design to use my will to access this (not my mind). I was also in a place of alignment with my request; I knew I needed a place to live to rebuild my life.

I refined my desire and visualized a townhome with a grassy area behind it where I could plant a garden of flowers, and a few days after my run (and my new declaration to God), a friend from the devotional community mentioned that she was in real estate. I asked her if she ever came across townhouses for rent.

"I'll call you when I return to my office," she said. "We don't typically handle rentals, but you never know."

She called me back almost immediately, somewhat shocked, as they did have a townhouse for rent. A client had just purchased a home and added the townhouse as a rental property. The townhouse was brand new! I went to see it the next day during my lunch hour.

Wow, this is just like what I saw in my vision, but even better! I thought. The townhouse featured a stream flowing alongside the property, nestled against a hill. The backyard offered open space leading to the stream.

"How much?" I asked.

"Well, it's more than you wanted to pay, and they don't take pets," she answered.

I would have to get a roommate, I thought.

"Okay, let me get back to you later today," I said.

I showed the townhouse to my mother after work.

"Oh, this is nice, honey, but how will you manage to afford it?"

"I'm going to get a roommate," I said.

"Who?"

"You!" I answered.

Change brought up a lot of fear for my mother, but with God's grace and Jan's guidance, we navigated her concerns and persuaded her to accept the move.

"Please ask the owner if we can pay $1,000 a month instead of $1,200, and let him know I have a cat," I told my real estate agent friend.

"He will never agree to any of this, Wendy. What are you thinking?"

"I'm thinking that this is my place. Just ask him, please."

The next day, she called and said, "Oh my God, he said yes! You have to put down a security deposit for the cat. I can't believe you pulled this off. What the hell are you doing in your life that you manifested this?"

"Among other things, I've been working with a psychic who has helped me confront my fears. She even identified issues my mother needs to address on a deeper level to prepare for moving in with me."

"Well, I need to talk to you more about this," my friend said. "My life sucks right now, and I definitely need to make some changes."

Miraculously, my brother and sister-in-law helped me pay off my debts, and Angelo provided me with the money for the deposit. I had never asked him for anything, even during our marriage. I always covered my own trips, clothing, and anything else I wanted.

We moved into our new townhouse at the beginning of May. With my bedroom window open, I could hear the sounds of the stream as it passed by; it was bliss. The outcome of my request to God while standing in the field that day was blooming beyond my expectations. The reason is that, in truth, I had no attachment to the outcome, so I went with the flow from a far more trusting place than I had ever been.

Part of what I read about visualizing something I desired was to avoid blocking what the Universe could send my way by limiting it with my own ideas about how it might happen; I just need to trust that what is for my highest good will come to fruition.

A few days after moving in, I attended a party where my friend Brenda introduced me to a man named Luke. She had talked about him over the years, as they had been romantically involved on and off. However, by the time of our meeting, they were just friends.

Luke and I chatted for a while, but I was tired from my recent move, so I left the party early. Several days later, he called me at work. At first, I didn't even remember who he was. He had to remind me that he was Brenda's friend from the party.

"How did you get my phone number?" I inquired.

"You mentioned where you worked, so I called and asked for you. Would you like to go out tonight?"

I felt tired and hesitant to go out, but he reassured me that we wouldn't be out late.

As I was driving back to my office after lunch that day, I suddenly realized that Luke was the man in the brown energy pattern in my vision! The shock of awareness was so great that I had to pull off the road to gather myself. I could not possibly imagine the reason this was happening.

I called Brenda as soon as I got back to work. "Brenda," I shouted into the phone, "you won't believe this! Remember when I told you about a dream I had, and a man's face appeared in the dream, filled with fear and brown energy? Well, that man is Luke. He just called and asked me out!"

"I don't know," she said. "Maybe he's your soulmate."

"I doubt that," I said. "He isn't really my type. He seems very lonely."

"Well, we will see about that!" she said. "Let me know how it goes."

I then called Jan. "I can send you a written reading on this," she mentioned. "You should receive it in a few days."

That evening, I went to Luke's house, intensely curious to discover why he appeared in my vision. We shared a drink and went out for dinner. I left right after our meal, as planned. He was a nice man, very good-looking with a beautiful smile and a mop of sandy hair. However, he was much more conservative than I, and certainly not interested in the esoteric or spiritual side of life. He drove a BMW, played squash, and belonged to a country club. I had grown up playing golf at my father's club and loved it, so I had no issue with any of that. I just had never dated anyone who owned his own home or had that sort of social status. At that time, I didn't see myself in that light, so I didn't understand why he had come into my life.

Jan's reading arrived a few days later and said, in part:

"It is also important for you to delve deeper into others, to feel their depths and not be deceived or confused by their emotions. Wendy, I felt that this statement pertained to your male friend you met at the party—the one you sensed was alone and depressed. Despite that, he is still full of life and vitality underneath and needs a reflection of that in his life. So, that may emerge for him, and you can be that reflection. They say you are on a new level of reading people, and you should recognize and work with that. Additionally, you are very close to meeting your companion. I see him standing right next to you, though not completely straight, which suggests that the alignment isn't complete and is in progress. However, I feel it is important for you to work with this other man."

On my next date with Luke, we went back to his house and sat by his pool for a while after dinner. His home was located at the end of a cul-de-sac, nestled in the woods. He sat in a chair next to me as we chatted and gazed at a beautiful tree, illuminated by landscape lights.

This would be a good time to look deeper into his soul to understand what he's really all about, as my guides suggested, I thought.

I took a breath and, respectfully and silently, asked for permission to take a look. A jolt coursed through me as I experienced the profound beauty of his being. He was full of life and sweetness. It shook me to my core. I had never felt anything like it.

Jan's reading suggested I go deeper into Luke and understand who he truly was. Asking for permission is important because it is a sacred act. I knew I needed to be mindful of seeking his higher self's permission so I could learn and experience what was genuinely in his heart and soul. It was a powerful lesson that taught me how "judging people" from my ego can be very deceiving; it's yet another tool in my toolbox.

It was so contrary to what I had observed on the surface that I felt profoundly humbled by the lesson. I sat there with tears streaming down my face, relieved it was dark so Luke couldn't see me crying.

Luke had been talking to me the whole time. Then, he suddenly got quiet and began sharing what he would love to do with his life. At that moment, he was a very successful president of a division in his company. He expressed his desire to live in the countryside and own a farm. He enjoyed working with the land. After elaborating on his dream for a while, he stopped abruptly and turned his head, looking at me with a surprised expression on his face.

"Wow, that's funny," he said. "I've never shared that with anyone!"

"Well, maybe you should try to pursue that dream since it's in your heart," I said.

"No, no, no, I can't do that."

I sensed his heart shut down, and that was that. We never spoke like that again, despite my efforts to encourage him to open up more than once.

We continued our relationship for a brief time. I was infatuated with him and could sense he felt the same way about me. However, it seemed he could not reconcile his heart with his mind. He was indeed a powerful mirror for me. He was emotionally closed off, which left me confused about whether we could develop a genuine romantic relationship. From my perspective, I couldn't comprehend how someone with such a magnificent soul and light within him would not want to embrace it. Then, I recalled my dream—the reflection of his face in the murk—and I realized that I, too, was closed off and afraid to open my heart to love. Well, I supposed my second visitation was nearing its end.

Meanwhile, my friendship with Brenda felt strained. I sensed she deeply resented my relationship with Luke. When I pressed her about it, she denied that it bothered her, but as Shakespeare said, "The lady doth protest too much, methinks." I realized she was actually sabotaging my relationship with Luke whenever she had the chance.

One night, in the place before dreamtime, my guides came to me. They brought me to a scene where I was speaking to Brenda about Luke. As I spoke, I felt in my emotional body what Brenda truly felt in hers. It was very painful. I was shocked by how much emotional pain she was experiencing over Luke. She wasn't over him at all. My guides reminded me of what they had said earlier about the importance of going deeper into others to feel their depths and not to be deceived or confused by their outward expressions.

I was the one who needed to make amends with my friend, even though I was hurt and angry with her. I could have avoided all of this if I had confronted her with the truth of what my gut was telling me. I had an opportunity to do so many months later, as we sat in her mother's kitchen after Luke and I had split up. Brenda told me that she had run into Luke but insisted once again that she was "over" him.

"Oh no, you don't," I said with a laugh, thankful for the opportunity to make amends. "You are *crazy* about him, and you have always been in love with him! I should have called you out on this from the beginning. It could have saved us both a lot of pain."

A big smile spread across her face as she cast her gaze downward. "Yes, you're right."

We both shared a good laugh.

CHAPTER 8

I'm Just Wild About Harry

"Have enough courage to trust love one
more time and always one more time."

—MAYA ANGELOU

As Luke and I approached our end, I recognized that my own
fear played a significant role in it, but I didn't know how to
address it. Man number two was inflicting a great deal of emotional angst on me, and I kept blaming him for it. I had prayed
for healing after leaving Angelo; I knew in my heart that this
was all part of the healing process, but it hurt like hell.

That July, my friend Carol and her husband invited me
to a housewarming party at their new home. Their friends
Harry and Debbie were also there. Carol disliked Debbie, as
she would constantly belittle Harry to his friends right in front
of him.

At the party, I was seated across from Harry while Debbie
spoke ill of her husband. Looking into Harry's eyes, I found
myself silently sending him the message, *If I can do it*—leave
my marriage with Angelo—*you can do it*. The thought came to
me out of nowhere.

Later that summer, Carol called and said, "Harry finally left Debbie!"

"No way! Well, he'll go back to her."

"No, no, he won't. I know he's finished with her."

"Well, more power to him. I hope it works out for him." I reflected on my own struggles in leaving my marriage.

By September, my relationship with Luke was already stagnant, so Carol invited me to a friend's wedding. She introduced me to her friend Geano, who would be my date. It wasn't easy to convince Carol to accept no for an answer, so I agreed.

We all had to drive to Philadelphia for the wedding, and we picked up Harry along the way, who was temporarily living with his sister after having left Debbie.

"Do you mind if I smoke?" Harry asked as he slid in next to me.

"Yes, I do mind!"

"Oh . . ." Harry said, clearly not expecting me to protest. He promptly lit his cigarette anyway.

At the wedding, while I danced with Geano, Harry leaned back in his chair, took a long drag on his cigarette, and gazed at me on the dance floor. Carol noticed the direction of his gaze and swatted his arm.

"What are you looking at? She's Geano's date. You leave her alone!"

"I thought I might ask her to dance!" Harry said with a broad grin.

"No, you will do no such thing, Harry. Besides, she's not your type anyway."

"Really? She looks like my type from where I'm sitting!"

"No, that's not what I'm talking about!" Carol continued. "She's into all that new age–type stuff—gurus, psychics, crystals, and things like that."

"Oh, I *see*," said Harry, pulling an even wider grin to taunt Carol for sport.

Carol's husband, Howard, became intrigued by the conversation, so he joined in.

"Harry, don't worry, ole boy. I'll discreetly ask her if she wouldn't mind giving you her phone number. A little new age never hurt anybody."

"Howard," Carol cautioned, "you fixed Harry up with his last wife. Look how that turned out. Stay out of this."

"Yes, dear," Howard said sarcastically, giving Harry a quick wink.

Well, Harry ignored Carol and asked me out, and I overlooked the cigarette incident and agreed. We had several dates that fall, but they were casual. I hadn't yet stopped seeing Luke and was still trying to determine if that relationship could work, while Harry was also dating Howard's secretary.

One Sunday, while Harry was visiting me, my phone rang.

"Wendy, it's Jan! Who is visiting you right now? Your companion is with you now! Who is it?"

"Uh . . . it's Harry."

"Wow," Jan responded. "I must be mistaken. It can't be Harry. He's nothing like you."

"Maybe you were wrong this time."

"I don't know. I was just sitting here with my kids, and I got this flash of your face and knew your companion was with you at this moment."

"Well, that would be Harry!"

Jan believed my soulmate would be someone who meditated, appreciated psychic work, listened to new age music, worked in a health food store, and never ate meat. Harry was wealthy, smoked, drank, drove an expensive car, and partied hard. How could Harry possibly be my soulmate? Plus, I still felt I was in love with Luke.

Harry and I continued to date, but I considered him a friend. I had no romantic interest in him at all. The thing about Harry that was so disarming to me, though, was that he was so damn "wiziwick." This is a marketing term from the early computer days that my brother shared with me. It means "what you see is what you get." When I explored Harry's emotional depth, it was not a deep, circuitous route. The beauty of his being was right on the surface. He wore his heart on his sleeve and wasn't capable of playing games. Because of this, he found it impossible to hide the fact that he was crazy about me. I took this knowledge very seriously. Plus, Carol said she would disown me if I ever hurt Harry.

I agreed to go out with him on Valentine's Day 1989, and he showed up at my door with a Winnie the Pooh stuffed animal. He had taken great pains to locate it because he knew I loved A. A. Milne's books. We went to a French restaurant on the waterfront in Philadelphia. He was so charming that I thought no woman would be safe with him—except for me since I was still holding onto Luke.

After dinner, Harry took me to a bar on the University of Pennsylvania campus to listen to a reggae band. We sat side by side in the bar, and he stole a quick kiss on the lips. A jolt of energy coursed through me, and I quickly got up and excused myself. While in the ladies' room, I told myself, "Get a grip. He's just your friend."

I decided to take the next day off from work to sort out my feelings. I called Luke and asked if we could get together on Saturday night for dinner. Then, I arranged a session with Jan.

"Wendy, you need to look Luke in the eye and ask him if he can love you," Jan told me. "All of this is about your feeling worthy of truly being loved, and until you confront this head-on, you will never be free to love another or be loved in the way you want."

The knot in my stomach was so intense that I felt nauseous.

"Jan, that is so awkward. I'm afraid he'll say no."

"Great! Then, you will know and stop playing games! You have been praying for your true companion. It's time to be courageous."

"Okay, okay, I know you're right." Boy, was I in uncharted waters.

Harry called and asked me out for Saturday night, and I told him I was going out with Luke. I could feel his heart sink, even though I knew he was still dating someone else, too. Harry could be a little devil, though, and I wondered if he would pull some kind of prank on me during my date with Luke. I wasn't in the mood for any pranks.

My mother absolutely adored Harry, so when the beautiful flower arrangement was delivered a few hours before Luke's arrival, she danced around the living room. The card said, "Forget me not!!"

"Honey, I love that Harry. He has such a great sense of humor and joie de vivre!" my mother said.

I was too nervous about my date with Luke and the task at hand to respond to her comment. Additionally, I was worried that Harry might have more surprises in his arsenal.

When Luke arrived, my mother chimed, "Luke, look at those flowers that arrived today. Aren't they lovely?"

I glared at her.

Luke never took the bait. He merely looked at the flowers with a dull expression and said, "Yeah."

I had a fleeting thought of Harry's laugh and how, if the situation were reversed, he would have pursued all manner of questioning.

At dinner, I ordered fish, and one taste was enough. "This fish isn't cooked right. It tastes awful!"

"Well, don't send it back and make a scene," Luke said. "Just eat it."

I had never made a scene in a restaurant in my life, and I thought, *Yes, Luke is right; I should eat it anyway and not make waves.*

Later, I had a chance to reflect on how powerful a metaphor that dinner was for me. As Luke and I sat on the couch in his living room, kissing and snuggling, bolstered by a glass of wine, I decided that the time was right to ask the question of my life.

"Luke," I said while gazing into his eyes, "could you love me?"

Jan had been very clear that I was to ask him in that exact way. "It's important that you ask him to love you and look deeply into his eyes. And *hear* the answer because you are truly worthy of being loved, fully and completely, nothing held back. You need to believe in this!"

I could feel that Luke was deeply attracted to me. Still, when I uttered the words, it felt as if someone else were saying them. I was so fearful.

He never answered my question and changed the subject. I followed him to his bedroom to make love, but I felt crushed. I tried to bring up the subject again, but he had shut down. That was that.

As he drove me back to my house that night, we remained mostly silent. I knew in my heart that I would never see him again. I adored him in many ways, but it was clear that he didn't want to love me or be in the kind of relationship I desired.

As painful, challenging, and scary as this evening was for me, I had asked for clarity, guidance, and truth. My emotions were in turmoil, but I was willing to move forward, not knowing what awaited me.

The whole notion of finding a "soulmate" was being adjusted for me as well. In truth, what was happening for me was quite simple. My intention after leaving my marriage and feeling crushed was to come into a better understanding and alignment so I was able to make choices that reflected who I was. Moving forward, I needed to *feel,* in my emotional body, the pain of my belief that I was not worthy of love.

Lying in my bed that night, I cried hard. It had taken a lot of courage for me to stand up for myself and ask to be loved. It hurt deeply to be soundly turned down. I thought about my ex-boyfriends and my ex-husband. I prayed for help and for the pain to go away, but somewhere in my heart, I felt the pain start to deepen into grief about my father and about the messages I internalized as a young child. I had truly believed that I wasn't good enough or worthy of being loved. This grief was not just about Luke; it encompassed so much more.

I let the tears flow for most of the night and tried not to push the pain and grief away. I prayed for the courage to face it so that I could bring in someone who truly wanted to love me, fully.

Jan wanted me to call her as soon as I could the next morning to let her know what happened with Luke.

"I feel awful. I was crying most of the night," I told Jan.

"It didn't go well with Luke, then?"

"No," I said as I sat on the floor of my bedroom, staring out the window at the bleak February sky. "He wasn't interested. I don't even think he understood the question. We were completely out of alignment. That was made painfully clear to me."

I explained to Jan my intense grieving process and how I had confronted deep pain regarding my father.

"Wendy, I know that it took a lot of courage and hurt like hell, but you moved some deep grief. That was necessary for your healing. Be good to yourself today. Your guides want you to know you *are* loved more than you know."

I hung up the phone, but it rang again immediately. It was 8:00 a.m.

"So, how was your date with Luke?" Harry's cheerful voice came through the receiver.

"Not great, Harry, and I'm really not in the mood to talk right now."

"Yeah, you don't sound great. Are you doing anything this morning?"

"I'm going for a run and then taking a walk around the lake."

"How about I meet you with some coffee?"

"I don't know, Harry. I'm not really good company this morning."

"That's okay. I will wait for you at the lake around ten, okay?"

"Suit yourself."

Near my townhouse by the stream was a beautiful lake nestled between the hills and surrounded by lush forests. You could walk the perimeter in about forty-five minutes. I loved walking my dog there, even in February. Along the trail, there was a spot on the bank where I enjoyed sitting and writing. Two trees with large trunks wound around each other like passionate lovers, their bark resembling human skin, and sinewy branches arching gracefully over the lake. They were magnificent trees—my "companion trees," I called them. To me, it was a sacred place where I could meditate and just be.

As I numbly walked along the trail to my companion tree, I looked up and saw Harry sitting under it with a thermos of coffee.

What is he *doing under* my *companion tree?* I wondered.

"Hey, I brought some coffee for you!" Harry said, bouncing up to greet me.

"Oh, thanks," I replied, without a hint of enthusiasm.

"How about we go out and get some lunch after you finish your walk? My car is parked in the lot by the boathouse."

"Yeah, okay, that would be fine, I suppose."

His effervescent openness began to feel refreshing and penetrate my feelings of annoyance.

At lunch, I shared a bit of what had happened the night before.

"Did you sleep with him?" Harry asked.

I looked into his eyes and answered, "Yes."

I could see the hurt in his eyes, even though he was still dating someone else. However, Harry's feelings were always apparent on his face.

Suddenly, I found myself wanting to spend more time with him, so I invited him to the U.S. Pro Indoor tennis championships in Philadelphia the following Saturday evening. We also went out for dinner during the week and talked on the phone a few times.

Our friend Howard (the very one who gave Harry my phone number) desperately wanted to know if Harry had "consummated" his relationship with me. He even went so far as to call Harry early one morning and pretend to be my father.

"Harry, this is Mr. Smith. Is my daughter with you?" Howard asked, disguising his voice.

"Uh . . . no, sir, your daughter is not here!" Harry said, stumbling over his words. As he had been jolted out of a deep sleep, he didn't catch on immediately.

Then, Howard burst out laughing.

"Oh, you fucking idiot, Howard. You scared the shit out of me! Why don't you just mind your own damn business?"

The boys had razzed Harry about "the hunt." The theory was that his ardent pursuit of me was only fueled by my lack of interest. Harry protested that they were wrong.

The movie *When Harry Met Sally* was playing in theaters, so we received a lot of ribbing from friends. Thank God it wasn't called *When Harry Met Wendy.*

When I got ready to meet Harry on Saturday, I packed an overnight bag. I felt it was time for me to open up to love. It wasn't an easy decision, but as I wrote affirmations about the kind of companion I wanted to walk with me in my life, I realized that Harry was right there, ready to be with me. And it scared the hell out of me. I was finally beginning to understand some of the lessons I had learned from the visitations of the first two men that Spirit had told me about. Was Harry number three?

While in the car with Harry, I quietly asked if he would mind my staying over at his house that night, ensuring he understood what I truly meant.

He swerved slightly off the road but quickly recovered with a gargantuan grin. "Oh, that would be fine, just *fine*." The light shooting from his being made me smile all the way down to my toes. What a difference a week makes.

That night, Harry and I drank a little too much, so we both quickly fell asleep without making love. Instead, we awoke in the middle of the night and finally consummated our relationship.

As soon as I felt Harry inside me, I knew absolutely that he was the one. Yes, he was a fine lover, but something else happened.

I "remembered" him. I'm not sure why it took an act of love-making to trigger this, but nevertheless, it did.

Early in the morning, in a profoundly uncharacteristic gesture for me, I whispered, "I love you," in Harry's ear.

"Oh . . . oh, I think I love you, too," Harry said. I could feel the shock wave going through him. "Umm . . . actually, I love you, too!" he blurted out, unable to stop himself.

"Yes, I know you do," I said to Harry, smiling.

I discovered a powerful truth. When you're aligned and have understood a lesson, there isn't much drama. What helped me learn this lesson? Trust and faith, along with the belief that when I know better, I can do better.

Our relationship continued to deepen. I knew we cared passionately for each other, but I was very worried about entering another marriage that I might come to regret or feel trapped in. Although we had not spoken of marriage, I was aware that it was the direction we were headed.

One night, alone at home in my own bed, I prayed to my guides for help in clarifying whether Harry was truly "my companion." I knew they would reveal what I couldn't or wouldn't see clearly as long as I asked for their assistance. I soon drifted off to sleep and shortly after awakened around 2:00 a.m. with a strong impulse to pick up a book from my shelf that I had purchased but not yet read—*The Bridge Across Forever* by Richard Bach.

I sat up and read enough chapters in the book to understand the concept of time travel concerning the future outcomes of decisions made now. The book described envisioning your future self to see how a decision might play out, given the current conditions and your understanding of life. Suddenly, I stopped reading, overwhelmed by that familiar need to close my eyes and surrender to the dreamtime. I felt my loving and benevolent teachers close ranks around my bed.

I turned off the light and was quickly transported to a vivid place. This was not a dream, as my senses were very acute, and I could feel my guides holding the space. In my mind, I was sitting on our couch, but it was in a smaller space like an apartment. My mother was sitting on the rocker, quietly doing her needlepoint. I looked around the room and recognized our furniture, but not the location. In my head, I asked my guides, "Why have we moved into a *smaller* place again?" I felt some panic rising, a doom and gloom scenario. But my guides and teachers were silent.

Then, I saw my future self coming through the front door of the apartment, absolutely beaming with happiness and light. "Hi, Mom," I said.

"Oh, hi, dear," my mother replied.

I looked at this future me and could truly see the joy on *my* face. I silently commented to my guides that the image was making me feel uncomfortable—the current me looking into the face of the future me. I was also still fixated on why my mother and I had moved. "What does this mean?" I asked again. "And what's the answer to my question about Harry?"

Once again, my guides remained silent. I knew they wanted me to answer my own question, as only I could. Then, they spoke to me. "It appears, dear one, that whatever choice you made, it has given you great happiness." Indeed, as I shifted back into present time, I carried that final feeling with me. The decision I made was the right one.

CHAPTER 9

Divine Intervention

"You cannot solve a problem with the
same consciousness that created it in
the first place."

—ALBERT EINSTEIN

In January 1990, Jamie moved back in with Angelo to change
schools for the ninth grade, as his dad's home was in a better
public school district. I would pick him up from school every
day and take him home to Angelo's house so that I could have
time to talk with my son. Although this gave me a lot of time
to spend with Harry at the start of our relationship, it was only
a few months before Jamie became completely out of control
and started failing in school. So, I told him to pack up his
things and move back in with me full-time.

One Saturday afternoon, shortly after Jamie had moved
back in with me full-time, we began with a disagreement over
some fireworks (of all things) that he had purchased without
my knowledge. The argument quickly escalated into a fierce
screaming match, during which Jamie cussed furiously at me.
I promptly instructed him to go to his third-floor loft room
and grounded him for the rest of the weekend. I could hear

him screaming and raging all the while trashing his room, so I went upstairs to talk to him with the intention of calming him down a bit.

He had smashed a hole in the wall with a bat. Then he turned and threatened me with it. I knew Jamie had some anger issues, but I suddenly realized that it was far worse than I thought. His face was filled with rage and pain as he started toward me and put me in a headlock.

I knew he would never actually hurt me, so a feeling of calm came over me. "Jamie, do you really want to do this to me?"

He let go and crumpled to the floor, dropped the bat, and stood on his bed, leaning against the wall, weaving back and forth. "I'm sick, Mom. I need to go to Deveraux. Can you call them?" Deveraux was a school for children with emotional problems.

Although I was deeply shaken, I felt an overwhelming love for my son in that moment and knew that it was essential for me to understand what was happening as clearly as possible.

"Jamie, I love you, and we're in this together. We'll figure something out. I'm not going anywhere."

I had a date with Harry that night, but, of course, I realized I would have to call him and cancel it to take care of Jamie. I was also experiencing a sharp dose of reality, thinking to myself that dating anyone was no longer an option until I got Jamie the help he needed.

Jamie and I were both afraid of what Harry might think and do if he learned what had occurred. Nothing like that had ever surfaced during my brief time with Harry.

When I tried to call him, though, the phone wasn't working. "I can't call Harry on his car phone to tell him not to come, but I'll explain when he gets here and ask him to leave," I reassured Jamie.

As I sat on my bed, feeling numb and scared, trying to process what had happened, Harry bounded through the front door. "Wen, where are you?" he said, cheerfully announcing his arrival.

"I'm upstairs in my bedroom," I replied, suddenly lacking the strength to go downstairs.

Harry sprinted up the stairs to my bedroom, halted in the doorway, and gazed at my face. At that moment, I realized how pale and distraught I must have appeared, yet I was powerless to conceal anything.

"What's happened?" His demeanor changed completely.

"Listen, Harry, I'm having some serious issues with Jamie, and I really need to be here with him. I tried to call you, but our phone line isn't working."

"Yeah," he said. "I tried to call you and couldn't get through."

Harry turned on his heels, walked back through the doorway of my room, and started pacing back and forth down the hallway. I sat still on the edge of my bed, aware that Harry was making a decision from his heart. I knew he often did that, but I had never "felt" his process so clearly. He suddenly bounded back up the stairs to the third-floor loft before I could stop him.

I heard him pause and survey the damage in Jamie's room. I closed my eyes. Jamie stood there with his eyes wide, not expecting Harry and not knowing what he would do or say. Harry then quietly put his arm around Jamie and said, "Okay, champ, how about you and I clean up this room? Then, I will take you and your mom out for pizza."

I didn't realize I had been holding my breath. I let out a deep exhale when I heard Harry's words. I looked up to the heavens and said, "Thank you, God. I know I can marry this man. Thank you!"

Harry came back down to my room and said, "Jamie and I are going to work on his room. Then, we'll go out for pizza. Is that okay? I'll have a contractor come over next week to fix the hole in the wall."

"Yes," I said. "Thank you."

Harry walked over and picked up the phone on my bedside table. We both heard a dial tone and briefly stared at each other . . . So the line was working again.

I was able to share Jamie's history and struggles at school with Harry. This man was incredibly authentic in his relationship with Jamie, and he didn't back down at all when Jamie challenged him.

I had been seeing a counselor to help me with the divorce, and the counselor believed that the diagnostic work done through the public school system was fraught with errors. She thought I should have Jamie undergo a full battery of tests from a private psychiatrist who specialized in learning disabilities and emotional issues.

Harry, wanting to examine his disastrous marriage, was also seeing a psychiatrist who provided us with the name of a doctor he believed was exceptionally skilled in psychological and educational diagnostics and only accepted patients through referrals. I was desperate at that point because I had no idea where Jamie would go to school in the fall. I had tried a few private schools the previous fall, but none of them had worked.

The diagnostic work was extensive and thorough, and the doctor also required me to take tests. At that point, Jamie had been spending his summer at a YMCA overnight camp, so we brought him home to work with the doctor on the testing. I also provided her with all the reports and information I had from kindergarten to ninth grade. Jamie had undergone numerous tests over the years due to his behavioral issues.

I received a call from the doctor on Sunday morning after she spent Saturday gathering all the information to create a comprehensive picture of Jamie.

"Wendy, I had to call you right away. Can you come over so that I can go over the results with you?"

"Yes, of course! Thank you." I was truly grateful that she had taken the time on a weekend to help us.

In this expert doctor's opinion, Jamie had been grossly misdiagnosed. He was not emotionally disturbed; he was learning disabled. In her twelve years of testing, she had never encountered a child who had achieved perfect scores on some of the IQ tests. She could not determine his true IQ because there was no existing measurement for it. Therefore, Jamie was actually categorized as gifted with a learning disability. He had social challenges related to the diagnosis, as did most children in that situation, but we finally knew how to proceed.

I was not in denial, but I did believe my child was emotionally disturbed. I cried all the way home, thinking about the damage to Jamie's psyche, his heart, his self-esteem—my God.

Finally, I was able to get the proper support. Testing for learning issues is very costly, though, and as I had learned, it requires a doctor of psychiatry with years of experience in educational diagnostics. There are hundreds of tests that can be given, and depending on the testing conditions, they can yield very different outcomes. The public school system simply couldn't afford to administer such extensive testing. Paying our new doctor's bill out of my savings was money well spent.

Accepting love and being loved created a chain of events that enabled me to get Jamie the help he needed. We found a new school for him in the fall that was specifically for gifted learning-disabled children.

Harry and I decided that we wanted to marry at some point, but he was in the midst of a very difficult divorce. I hadn't even formally filed for divorce, so I decided it was time to face that music as well.

Jan had admonished me for not confirming to Angelo that our marriage was over. I knew he still held out hope, even after three years, that I would somehow return to him. So, I took a deep breath, informed Angelo that our marriage was over, and that I was filing for divorce. Well, that's when things got ugly.

We battled over child support in the courts (even after our divorce was settled). As painful and stressful as it was, I was still glad that I took the steps to resolve the situation. It took over a year to be finalized.

While at work in August of 1990, Harry called me from a courthouse pay phone.

"Honey, Debbie finally signed the divorce agreement. I had to give her a lot of money, but it was worth it. It's over! Will you marry me?!"

"Ah, Harry, don't you want some downtime for a while? There's no rush."

"No, I want to marry you right away. I don't need any time."

I knew Harry was serious and very confident, despite the difficulties of his first marriage. I thought about how I had appreciated my last three years of single life, but I decided to simply follow my heart.

"Yes, of course, I will marry you!"

"Great! I'll see you tonight after work. I'm not going back to the office today!" he said.

And so, it began . . .

We decided to get married at St. David's Church, a small, Colonial-style stone church with white shutters framing rounded windows with multi-divided panes. Built in 1715 by Welsh colonists who settled in that area of Pennsylvania, it sits next to a historic graveyard where the likes of Anthony Wayne, major general of the American forces during the Revolutionary War, are buried, along with various members of Harry's family over the generations. His family descends from Elisha Boudinot, president of the first Continental Congress.

Although I had attended services at the church before, when I went in to look it over as a venue for my marriage, I closed my eyes and sensed something very special about it. In reading its history, I discovered something that intrigued me: "With the coming of the Revolution in the colonies, a rapidly swelling wave of resentment against the Church of England arose among the patriots of the congregation." Anthony Wayne was one of the patriots in the congregation at the time, yet the church building provided refuge for soldiers on both sides. I found it extraordinary that it was not destroyed like many old churches in the area and that, despite the bitter resentments created by the war, it had remained "neutral."

The church could only accommodate one hundred people, so my guest list would work. There was just one thing left to do. Harry called the church and spoke to Steve, the rector. Harry's first wedding had taken place at the chapel across the street, which was built to serve a growing congregation over the years. It could hold two hundred to three hundred people.

Several days later, the phone rang. It was Rudy, the church's minister. "Wendy, I spoke with Steve, and he felt very strongly that you and Harry cannot be married in the church since Harry was married here before. He doesn't want to set that type of precedent. I'm so very sorry." Rudy was an old friend of Harry's family; he had performed Harry's first wedding ceremony.

"Rudy, may I come in and meet with you? I want to tell you a story about Harry and me. When I'm finished, if you still believe we shouldn't be married at St. David's, I will understand," I said.

"Yes, of course, that would be fine, but I really don't think Steve will change his mind."

When I arrived for our meeting, Rudy led me to a small office that barely held a desk and two chairs. He offered me the more comfortable chair with a high back and two armrests, while he took the smaller chair.

"Rudy, I want to share with you how I knew marrying Harry was the right thing for me. As you know, I have been married before, too, and I had great concerns about getting into another marriage."

I continued and told Rudy about the moment my prayer to God was answered regarding whether or not I should marry Harry. I shared the incident with Jamie—the day we fought and he destroyed his room—and how Harry acted that evening. As I recounted my story, I became aware of a powerful shift of energy in the room, flowing through the top of my head and spreading throughout my body. Although I could feel it intensifying, I remained focused on the telling. Often when I share the story, I begin to cry, but I didn't that day.

When I finished, Rudy stood up abruptly and said, "Wow, there is a lot of spirit in this room! We're clearly going to have to rethink this. I will have a word with Steve."

At that, he stepped back and tripped over the chair, stumbling into the door. I heard him mumble to himself as he turned and left.

"Thank you so much, Rudy," I called to him. "I appreciate your help."

The phone call from Rudy came several days later. "Wendy, I spoke with Steve, and he changed his mind! You and Harry may be married in the church. He said I could not officiate the ceremony, however, as I did Harry's first wedding. Lou Mills, our other minister, will officiate. Steve has also requested that you and Harry meet with Lou for premarital counseling."

I loved Lou from the moment I met him. He was a strong, intelligent, and passionate Yank. His wife, a therapeutic counselor, helped update our wedding vows to reflect a more balanced male/female bipartisan agreement.

After our wedding rehearsal, Lou baptized me in the church. As he touched my head with the holy water, I felt a moment of Divine Grace and bliss. When I opened my eyes to look into Lou's face, he smiled and said, "Wow, that was powerful!"

I beamed back at him and said, "Yes, I wasn't expecting that!"

I had always felt that church rituals were void of true spiritual enlightenment. Perhaps it was I who had been lacking in inner spiritual insight, and the deeper connection to God that I eventually cultivated allowed me to experience the essence of baptism more profoundly.

When I awoke on the morning of our wedding—a balmy seventy-two-degree early March day—I said a prayer of gratitude. It was going to be a lovely day in many ways. I also prayed that I would remain conscious and strong throughout the ceremony without sobbing as I experienced the grace and power of the union. I wanted dignity to shine in my character that day!

The ceremony was set to begin at noon. Harry was so nervous that he arrived at the church over an hour early.

As the wedding march began, Jamie walked me down the aisle. Standing next to Harry at the altar, I kept sensing a "presence" next to me on my right side. It felt very distinct yet soft and cloudlike. In the video of our wedding, you can see me glancing over my right shoulder, trying to see if something was there.

There was a heating grate on the floor, and I thought perhaps I was standing near it. But it wasn't anywhere close to my spot. When Lou began, I felt once again that a great deal of spirit was present in our little church. At one point, the big double doors blew open with a crash, and candles flickered wildly. It was quite dramatic! Someone jumped up and shut the doors, and I saw Lou catch his breath as he continued with the ceremony.

My friend Carol's son, who was seventeen at the time, asked me after the ceremony, "What was going on in that church? The doors crashed open; the candles were flickering on and off. It was unbelievable!" He had attended the church as a child and had never seen anything like that.

"I guess there was a lot of spirit in that church, Seth," I remarked.

CHAPTER 10

Chop Wood and Carry Water

"Your pain is the breaking of the shell
that encloses your understanding."

—KAHLIL GIBRAN

After Harry and I were married, I continued meditating, but I didn't listen to holy discourse or spend as much time with the devotional community. However, when I received a call from a friend who said they were hosting a woman who channeled Spirit, I was very excited to attend the gathering.

The channeler, Robin Velez, introduced herself and explained her work. She stated that she would close her eyes, open herself up inside, and allow Spirit to come. She mentioned that she channeled entities who called themselves Isaiah and the Group. I was thrilled to have someone like this in my own town!

Afterward, I scheduled an appointment for a private session with Robin. I wanted to discuss that Jan didn't approve of Harry or my new life, and I wasn't sure how to handle it. Isaiah (channeled by Robin) told me I would no longer be working with Jan because my new life was triggering her. He said that it was extremely important, however, for me to call her and thank her sincerely from my heart for all the work she had done with me and to bless her genuinely. I had felt very hurt and annoyed with Jan, but I called her anyway.

"Jan, I want to thank you for all you have done for me—the help and understanding, the bringing of information from my spirit guides. Thank you." I could feel the shift of true gratitude and love flowing through my voice, and I was surprised because I started the conversation still feeling betrayed and hurt. I knew Jan could feel the blessing of grace as well, and I could tell she was touched and grateful for my call. However, I also knew that when I hung up, I wouldn't speak with her again.

"When the student is ready, the teacher will come." That is a powerful and true axiom, and my new teachers have entered my life through the work of Robin Velez.

For me, this marked the beginning of a new and deeper process of healing and spiritual growth. How fitting that I met Robin through my friends in the devotional community.

Working with my new teachers was exhilarating and deeply challenging. I "knew" they could see all of my being—past, present, and possible options for the future. They also knew what was embedded in my heart and were able to slowly guide me deeper into my life, helping me to see and feel all aspects of my being with the highest integrity. The intimacy, love, and trust that I have built with them over the years has helped me navigate through significant resistance and fear.

During the summer after our wedding, I became pregnant. We were very excited! I didn't know if I would be able to conceive after so many years of using birth control. Since I was turning forty, I had a test for birth defects. After the test, I experienced prolonged bleeding, so I decided to stop working earlier than expected and rest before the birth.

During the latter part of my eighth month, Jamie struggled significantly in school. He created plenty of drama and distress with one of the teachers, which required me to go to the school for several interventions. Fortunately, the headmistress and teaching team were very patient with Jamie.

I also had a very stressful court date with Angelo, as our battle over payment of Jamie's school tuition escalated. I had an appointment with my OB/GYN, Lynn, on Thursday of that same week, and I mentioned to her that I was having a stressful week and had not felt the baby move for a little while. I saw a look of concern flash across her eyes as she placed her stethoscope on my very large belly to listen. After a few moments, without saying a word, she grabbed my hand and pulled me off the table with some force. Gripping my hand tightly, she whisked me into another room with an ultrasound machine. I quickly lay on the table with a great feeling of dread. Wordlessly, Lynn moved the ultrasound wand around with her right hand and clutched her stomach with her left. I realized that she, too, was feeling distress.

I could feel her thoughts. "You don't want to have to say this to me," I said to her. Lynn was an old friend of Harry's, and her parents were dear friends of Harry's father and stepmother. They all went way back.

139

Lynn paused for a moment. Then, looking away from the monitor to face me, she said, "Wendy, there is no heartbeat."

"What can we do to save the baby?" I asked, unwilling to comprehend her statement.

"Wendy," Lynn began gently, "your baby is no longer alive. There's nothing we can do. Even if it had happened just now on the table, I wouldn't have had enough time to prep you and do a caesarean section. Let's go into my office so that you can call Harry to come and get you."

Looking into my eyes, Lynn touched my arm and said, "I'm so sorry." Then she gave me a hug.

After Harry arrived, Lynn took me back into her examination room and gave me an injection that would induce labor. "Can't you just schedule me for a caesarean section? Why do I have to go through a vaginal birth if the baby is no longer alive?" I asked.

I felt a deep dread about the arduous process of labor, knowing the baby would be stillborn.

"Wendy," Lynn said, "caesarean sections are very serious operations. If you choose to get pregnant again, it's much healthier to give birth vaginally."

So, it was agreed. Although it was Lynn's day off, I would come in the next morning to the maternity ward, and another doctor in her practice would attend my delivery. Unfortunately, the next day was also Valentine's Day.

Lynn asked if I wanted some Valium to ease the shock.

"No, thank you. I need to feel this," I said. I couldn't imagine that any amount or form of medication could ease my suffering.

When Harry took me home, the ride was quiet. We were both devastated and numb. Not having the faintest idea of what to do with myself after we got home, I stood in our bedroom, contemplating whether I should do some laundry or housework. I touched my abdomen, large and firm, but our baby was no longer moving. I sat down and began to sob. *This is entirely my fault*, I thought. *I let the stress of my court date with Angelo and Jamie's infractions with his teachers affect me. I should have realized this could harm our baby!*

The following day, I went to the hospital and gave birth. I didn't receive any heavy drugs because they said I could go home quicker. After the birth, a grief counselor came in and asked if I wanted to hold the baby before he was taken away for an autopsy.

"No," I mumbled. "I . . . I can't do it." I was afraid I would split into a thousand pieces if I held my precious stillborn child. I felt guilty, of course, and judged myself a bad mother for that decision, but I rolled over onto my side and closed my eyes.

I was awakened by Lynn, who had come in specifically to see me. "Wendy, how are you doing?" I opened my eyes to find her sitting on a stool, inches from my face.

"Lynn, I want to go home. Can you get me released?"

Her face was so beautiful, and her eyes sparkled with compassion. Her presence brought me comfort.

"Let me see what I can do," she whispered.

She was painfully aware that the joy of the live births happening around us in the maternity ward on Valentine's Day was excruciating for me.

She managed to get me released, with the promise that I would stay in bed for four days and not drive for at least a week.

My friend Angela flew in on the red-eye to help us. That evening, as I lay upstairs in bed, Angela helped Harry with dinner. I could hear pans crashing and a glass breaking. Angela came upstairs to ask me something, and I took one look at her top and said, "My God, you look like you've been in a war zone!" She had béarnaise sauce, mashed potatoes, and what I thought might be a remnant of a martini splashed across her lovely light-colored blouse.

"Oh my God, Wendy, I know Harry is upset about the loss of your baby, but he is downright dangerous in the kitchen tonight. I can't get out of his way fast enough!"

It made me laugh.

When I went out in public, I still looked pregnant. It was devastating when someone asked when I was due. I probably wouldn't have left the house at all for a while, but we were in the process of building a new house farther out in the country.

I scheduled a session with Robin ten days after I got out of the hospital. When I called to make the appointment and shared with her what had happened, she said, "Wendy, I'm so sorry to hear of the loss of your baby. All spiritual rhetoric aside, it really sucks."

"Yeah, that about sums it up for me," I said with a deep sigh.

"I'm surprised you want a session. A lot of clients blame me or Spirit when they encounter a devastating loss, saying that we should have been able to tell them it was going to happen or prevent it altogether."

"No, no, I understand that is not how it works; I need comfort and a deeper understanding of what occurred."

Isaiah helped me understand why the loss of our baby could not be foretold. Predictions come from the future, and they can change due to free will. I realized how important it is to embrace the moment and live fully in each moment, because that is all there truly is.

Depending on my actions, the future will change accordingly. That was a hard way to learn the lesson, but I got it. Spirit assured me that it was nothing I had done. There were some unfinished past life patterns with the soul of the baby, and I needed to endure. After my session with Robin, the guides asked me to do some energy work on my heart and my uterus. This life that had been growing inside me, as he grew and poked me with his extremities, is indescribable, albeit uncomfortable in the later months. But we were one; he was growing off my body, I was nourishing him, and we were intertwined body, mind, and soul. To have this ending felt like a part of my being was being ripped from me. The grief was torture. The channel was, as always, direct and honest, but with so much love, Isaiah spoke to me on several occasions about some aspects of the past life patterns I shared with this soul. I also understood that free will could have dictated a different outcome should the soul have chosen that which would have served the highest good. I was beginning to understand how multidimensional my existence was.

For quite a while, I felt raw around people. I couldn't look anyone in the eye because I felt so vulnerable, as though I would break apart and never return to wholeness. A dear friend who had been through a number of miscarriages—one as late as six months—looked at me one day and said, "Wendy, you are *not* grieving the death of your baby. You're pushing it away."

I knew she was right. I just didn't know what else to do but keep praying for help. I often awoke in the middle of the night, stared at the ceiling, and cried. I guess I needed to grieve the loss in the stillness of the night.

I awoke one night, trying to think about the many things I was grateful for in my life, including the joy of my marriage to Harry. I lay there reflecting on our marriage ceremony and all of the blessings and spirit present in the church that day. I thought about the feeling I had of a being or spirit pressing against my right shoulder in the church to the point that I felt as though I were standing on a heating grate. "Who was that?" I quietly spoke out to the night. The answer was immediate and clear: "It was Jesus."

Tears began to stream down my face. I understood. Jesus, the man on Earth whom Christians revere as the Son of God, had shed his human body and ascended. He was an ascended being whose presence was omnipotent, not bound by earthly dimensions or perspectives. As I lay there, I thought about that day on the hill and my angry insistence that Jesus appear and tell me what the hell was going on in the world and why it was so screwed up. Was my experience at the wedding connected to that day? Exhausted, I drifted off to sleep.

The emotional floodgates finally opened when I wrote a letter to my deceased son. Then, I wrote a letter to my father in my journal—one that I would not send but only write for myself—about how much I had missed having him in my life.

As I deeply grieved the loss of a father, was I also grieving the disconnect from God that I felt?

I sat with the grief, trusting my inner guidance that the emotion would not drown me. I just had to acknowledge it, feel it, and breathe through it.

Several weeks later, as life had tentatively settled into a rhythm, I found myself sinking back into a deep funk. I still hated going out because I looked pregnant. I cursed my body for not having bounced back as it had in my twenties after Jamie was born.

My mother called and asked me if I would take her to the hairdresser. Her hairdresser was far enough away that I didn't expect to run into anyone I knew, so I picked up my mother and drove her to her appointment. As I sat on a padded bench at the front of the beauty parlor, I looked up to see a woman walking toward me who had been on the board of my former employer. Beth had a wonderful family, and I had always been very fond of them. But I thought to myself, *Shit.*

"Oh, Wendy, hi! Look at you! I heard you were pregnant. When are you due?"

My face turned ashen, and I looked down, feeling the onset of tears. "I had a stillborn birth a few weeks ago." I barely managed to get the words out, feeling the powerful dread of falling completely apart.

Beth quickly set her purse down, sat beside me on the bench, and took my hand in hers. "Wendy, I'm so sorry to hear that."

After a brief pause, she quietly said, "Wendy, I also gave birth to a stillborn baby—my first pregnancy. And you know my daughter, Kim? She had a stillborn child her first pregnancy as well."

The pain in my heart was so overwhelming that I could barely look up at her.

Still holding my hand, she looked silently up to God, then back at me. "You know, I'm not usually in this part of town, but I had a flat tire right in front of this hairdresser! So, I came in to see if I could use their phone. Isn't that a coincidence? God works in mysterious ways."

Oh, yes, he does, I sighed wearily to myself, knowing in my heart that her appearance was no accident.

"Listen," she said, "the truck is here to fix my tire. Here's Kim's phone number. She's part of a support group for parents who have had stillborn children. You're not alone! Give her a call."

I could feel my beloved guides helping me. It was hard, but I just kept putting one foot in front of the other. I might try to run, but I wasn't going to hide.

Several months later, I called my stepmother, Patricia, to ask her a question. During our conversation, she suddenly, without warning, asked me, "Where are the pots and pans I gave you?"

"Wh-what?" I stuttered, completely taken aback. She had given them to me in 1982. It was an old set of Paul Revere cookware pans that she had already owned for many years. Trying to think of where they were, I realized they must have gone to my mother's house when I moved in with Harry prior to our wedding.

"I think they're at my mother's house," I said.

"Your mother's house!" she said. Suddenly, her tone was full of the hatred she had harbored toward my mother for years. "You go over there *now* and get them. Do you hear me?!" She launched into a tirade that was vicious and mean-spirited in every sense of the word. I knew all too well how she could turn on me in an instant, but following such a devastating loss, I was crushed. I mumbled something to her and hung up on her.

Harry was dumbfounded.

"Well," I said, after telling him the story, "if she wants her thirty-year-old pots and pans, she can drive up from West Virginia and pick them up."

The next day, my father called me. "Wen, I'm in a terrible mess here. Patricia is really on a tear about those pots and pans. I need you to call her, apologize, and mail them down to us right away."

Through my grieving process and journaling, I gained significant clarity about my role as an adult in the lives of my father, stepmother, and mother. I came to recognize the manipulations I endured due to my father's attempts to keep Patricia happy at all costs. Throughout my life, I trembled with fear whenever Patricia became upset about something. My father would become very uptight, and I felt compelled to do whatever it took to make her happy, even if it meant ignoring my own inner voice. Striving to keep her on her pedestal meant sacrificing my own self-worth.

I took a breath and said, "Dad, she is a vicious and jealous woman. I'm no longer going to participate in this. You married her; you deal with it. The pots and pans will be at the end of my driveway. Drive the eight hundred miles to come and get them. I will hear no more about it!"

Finally, I was able to respond to my father in a healthier way. At that point, I truly didn't care if I ever saw him again. But he knew I was right and understood my position.

Of course, it was about much more than "pots and pans." New clarity helped me understand my role in the dynamics involving my father, mother, and stepmother. Spiritually, I knew that we had all been together in previous lifetimes and that I had chosen to incarnate through my parents for my growth and healing. However, living it and feeling it, even in the light of my understanding, was a monumental challenge. It required me to pray for guidance and work at taking the high road. As Robin said, "Sometimes, it just sucks."

I was compelled to continue confronting the truth in many areas. In a subsequent session with Robin, Isaiah pointed out: "You say to us internally that you will have another child, but you're vacillating. So, you need to sit with this, not just for three months before you make a choice"—when I had been told my menstrual periods would probably start again—"but at least four to six months before you make a choice. This must be a committed decision, Wendy, knowing it will not take *from* your life, but give *to* it."

Then, the channel's voice became very quiet. "Do you understand that? You must also understand that the grief process about the loss of this child is the grief of loss of the self. *Period.*"

I realized they were right, and I took a look at the truth about wanting another child. Jamie had been extremely challenging for me. I recognized the grace of having him, as his difficulties made me step up, conduct research, and learn how to help him. I discovered how to trust my gut when I was bullied by teachers who were frustrated with him and unable to admit they didn't know what to do. But I wasn't sure if I could raise another difficult child should the genetic roll of the dice spin in that direction. I reconciled it all as best I could. Before I knew it—just five months after my stillborn birth—I was pregnant again.

Later, while sitting in Lynn's office after an exam, she paused and looked at me. "Wendy, you and Harry are going to be nervous wrecks throughout this pregnancy. Even though the death of your baby was not due to your age but to an umbilical cord that kinked and cut off oxygen, I'm going to treat this as a high-risk pregnancy."

I decided to use my meditation practice to stay as calm as possible. Even after all my years of practice, though, my efforts were mediocre at best. Why, at the first sign of deep trouble in my life, would I abandon what could help me the most?

Despite the stress, fear, anger, and a long nine months, our son arrived safe and sound. We had planned to name our first child Tucker. Some people felt it wasn't a good idea to name our new child Tucker as well. However, after the delivery, the nurse brought my tiny newborn son to me and left. As I held him in my arms, I spoke out loud, addressing his spirit.

"Well, it seems the only name that your father and I truly agree upon is Tucker. That was the name we were going to use for our baby who died, so if you have a problem with the name, please give me a sign." The room became very still and bright.

I could feel the energy crackle with such peace and a loving consciousness. Nothing was spoken back to me, but I knew the name Tucker would be just fine.

After the birth, Tucker was healthy, but my nerves were frayed. I felt as if every cell in my being belonged to someone else. I spoke with Isaiah through Robin a couple of weeks after Tucker was born.

"Now, with the child himself, the fear of his passing will alleviate as you become more comfortable here with him. Do you understand that?"

"You mean the fear of death around him?" I was so filled with terror that I wanted to ensure I understood every word clearly.

"Yes, this is normal due to what happened. Also, this child has experienced a stillborn event and a crib death in other lifetimes."

"Oh God, I've been worried about that."

"Yes, you can keep him in your room until the third or fourth month. Then, you can move him into his own room because that fear is *very* strong in you. We want to alleviate it so you can find some peace here. This has been a tremendous healing for you, Wendy, not just regarding your first son and this newborn but also for you as a woman, allowing you to experience pleasure and completeness in your life. This is the time for your healing, and this is why we wanted to talk to you. Everything will be all right now. The child will be fine; he has much to give to this world, this little one. Just make sure that he has a balance of both a father and a mother here."

Addressing the multidimensional issues provided me with some comfort, and I understood that Tucker would be fine. They had ensured that I comprehended that. Still, even with all the grace, wisdom, guidance, and—most importantly—love, the experience of losing a child sent a cataclysmic ripple through my being. The love of my husband, the support of dear friends and family, and the understanding that I could always seek counsel from Spirit helped me through those days.

When Tucker was two years old, I was fortunate to meet Reverend Alex L. Orbito. Alex was from the Philippines, where he grew up in a family devoted to spiritual healing and mediumship. I had seen a documentary on his healing works many years prior to meeting him. A friend who lived in Virginia Beach and worked with the Edgar Cayce Foundation was helping to run a two-day healing seminar with Alex over the Fourth of July. As my friend entered the room for Alex to work on her, he looked up at me and motioned for me to enter as well.

To my friend Claire, Alex asked, "She is your friend, yes?"

"Yes, may she watch you work?" Claire asked.

"Yes, of course!"

I was overjoyed; this was a dream come true for me! As Claire lay on the table and Alex prayed, I instantly became aware of a powerful shift in the energy of the room. Tears started streaming down my face as I felt the energy of grace and love flow into my heart.

I looked over at Alex and saw his hand open up the skin on Claire's abdomen and pull some sort of dark matter out of her. He placed it in the bag one of his assistants was holding.

Claire quickly glanced at me and said, "Wendy, this doesn't hurt, and there is no pain—just an odd sensation."

Then, it was my turn to lie down on the table. I was nervous but felt safe. Alex placed his hand first on my abdomen, and it felt like a fine grade of sandpaper as the tissue separated and he began extracting some dark tissue from my body. He then moved up to my throat area, followed by my third eye.

My father and stepmother had driven up from West Virginia for a visit, and when I returned home, I noticed a blue aura surrounding my father's body. I felt that the healing session with Alex had heightened my psychic abilities.

About a year later, Alex visited a friend's home not far from where I lived to conduct a one-day healing session. His appearance wasn't advertised except through word of mouth. After my time with him, I waited with others who wanted to meet Alex once he finished his sessions. He entered the room and sat on the couch next to me, taking my hand in his as he casually spoke with all of us. I could see that he was drained and needed a few moments to recharge.

Turning to me while still holding my hand, Alex said, "I can remove the 'dis-ease' from people, but often it returns because I cannot remove the karmic, past-life, or current-life reason they have drawn the dis-ease to themselves in the first place."

I knew that everything I do or did in all my lifetimes is imprinted, something like storing things in the cloud. It's all part of who I am—the good and the bad. It's all recorded, not for judgment day purposes but for growth. This was not an easy concept for me to grasp because who the hell wants to draw cancer to them or the death of a baby? Seriously! It sounds ludicrous. But I did understand what Alex was speaking about.

In order to heal ourselves, we must understand where disease comes from and how it relates to us in the present, and what it has to teach us.

Good reminder—note to self, I thought.

CHAPTER 11

What's Love Got to Do with It?

"Do you choose love or fear? Unconditional love would choose both by bringing our fears within love and finding
out what they have to offer."

—*CEANNE DeROHAN IN*
RIGHT USE OF WILL

When Tucker was four years old, we had the opportunity to
move to Santa Fe, New Mexico. I had spent nearly my entire life
in southeastern Pennsylvania, with its rolling green hills carved
out with large stands of forests. It was a monumental change to
leave behind the trees I loved, sentinels of a soft energy that made
me feel small, safe, and connected to the earth. Even on a cellular
level, I could sense the shift caused by the move.

Even though moving was challenging on many levels, Harry
and I felt excited to be living in the Southwest. Santa Fe was a
cacophony of colors, smells, sounds, and a visual extravaganza
of mountains and high chaparral. Nothing I had read or pic-
tured about Santa Fe did it justice. The energy radiating from
the earth was a spiritual accelerant pulsing through me. The
clean air, infused with the scent of pinyon pine trees and earth,

nestled against the Sangre de Cristo Mountains (the south-ern tip of the Rockies) and the bright turquoise skies. I was standing on the earth, touching the sky with nothing to cover, protect, or hide me like my beloved Pennsylvania trees. I was exposed.

Just after I moved to Santa Fe, I had several sessions with Isaiah and the group channeled by Robin, who had by then changed her name to Amaya. The following is an excerpt from one of our conversations.

Because you are feeling so much anxiety, you are not allowing your-self just to be. You understand? You are not allowing yourself to just be with the information, whatever that moment is holding for you. You are not allowing yourself to breathe into it. You are run-ning ahead, trying to fix it because it makes you uncomfortable. It is understandable because you really love God and want to do the best you can, and you really want to be perfect here.

What we are trying to say to you with all those words is . . . it's not a time to be perfect; it's a time to relax. It's time to learn what true unfoldment is about. It's not an analytical process, which is where you like to go. It's a process of the soul, of the spirit; an experiential process, an energetic process that encompasses or incor-porates the mind, the heart, and the emotions. Do you understand?

So you need to learn to come from another way; it's not about doing but about experiencing, expressing, being, and allowing. Do you understand? This means doing is involved—you have to walk around, eat, breathe, sleep, and interact. You have to create, and your creation must come through action, right? But it's really about relaxing into intention and healing your fear of other human beings. This is significant for you; you are in a totally new place with no role models. When you were on the East Coast, you felt safe because you blended in. Out here, you don't. Out here, you literally have to change yourself; don't expect the information around you to change.

This is very normal for the Southwest. You knew, when out here, that the energy would confront you with your true transformation, and that is what is going on; you are being asked to change.

At the time, I was struggling with a great deal of fear—fear about money, Jamie's future, finding the right school for Tucker, and securing a house. I was also concerned about not discovering my true calling and not being "spiritual enough."

Whenever I had these sessions with Spirit, they would talk to me, but I also knew they were working on me energetically. I could feel the work, and honestly, the whole thing was very intense for me. The caveat was the *love*, the deep heart connection I have with these magnificent beings; as I walked through hellfire, they had my back, never leaving my side. Because they, too, had at one time or another walked this same path, when they were incarnate on Earth. I knew that with every fiber of my being.

Well, I had clearly come to the Southwest to do some very deep healing.

When I signed Tucker in at his new preschool, I must have looked terribly harried. Another mother said, "Oooh, you're new here. Don't worry. You'll settle down. There's lithium in the water here!" Her Scottish accent and the twinkle in her eye instantly endeared her to me. She soon became a dear friend and a grounding force in my new town.

Meanwhile, the situation with Jamie was not helping me to alleviate stress. While in college, he developed anxiety and depression that were so disabling that we pulled him out of school and sent him to a well-known psychologist and MD. He was first prescribed an anti-anxiety medication like Valium, then an antidepressant and OxyContin sometime after that to treat headaches. It was a brand-new drug at that time.

Afterward, Jamie's behavior became increasingly bizarre. He was living in Pennsylvania with his father, and Angelo didn't know what to do. I had noticed that Jamie's personality always changed dramatically when he was given some kind of pain medication, so I began to have my suspicions. In the past, I always ensured that he stopped taking the pills as soon as the pain subsided.

Jamie confided in me that although his prescription for OxyContin was for thirty days, he was obtaining a refill every two weeks and consuming more than necessary. The doctor never reviewed her records to see when she had issued the last prescription, despite several inquiries from pharmacists. This practice had persisted for about eighteen months. I asked her about the potency of OxyContin, and she informed me that it was utilized for pain management in the final stages of cancer.

"Why in God's name are you giving him this drug?"

"I sent him to a pain clinic for headaches, and it's what they recommended," she said.

"I want to suspend Jamie's sessions with you, and please don't write him any more prescriptions for OxyContin," I told her.

Clearly, Jamie's so-called "treatment" plan was an epic failure.

My next call was to my old boyfriend William, who had been through many drug treatment programs. He made phone calls for me and found a two-week detox program for Jamie. Unfortunately, that was the limit set by our insurance company for recovery programs at that time. We knew two weeks was likely not enough but we had to move forward.

William meticulously prepared me for everything I might encounter when I flew to Philadelphia to pick up Jamie and take him to rehab. William informed me about all the squirrely tricks Jamie would pull and how I should handle each one. God bless William because he was spot on. Jamie's behavior was textbook. He dosed himself with all the drugs he had left, he needed underwear and socks, and he hadn't eaten.

I took him out to lunch, and at the end of the meal, I said, "Jamie, I have a plane to catch, and I'm dropping you off at rehab at six. *Period.*"

William desperately wanted Jamie to continue in a two-year program. I knew he was right, but I also knew, sadly, that Jamie would never agree to it. He was twenty-three by that time and free to turn down treatment. He had absolutely no idea how addictive opiates could be. In his mind, two weeks would surely do the trick.

The woman at the front desk of the rehab said, "We've had a lot of people in our program recently detoxing from OxyContin. It's an escalating problem. It's a new drug on the market, and it seems to be highly addictive."

As I knew would be the case, Jamie was in for a rude awakening. His first two weeks in rehab were only the beginning of many years of struggling and suffering with the disease of addiction. His life has gone through a series of unravelings as he has failed to grasp recovery in a number of treatment programs.

For me, the stress of watching my beloved child destroy his life and both his mental and physical health took a tremendous toll on my own health. In the winter of 2002, I was informed that all of my reproductive organs were diseased, necessitating a complete hysterectomy. By the grace of God, I didn't have cancer, but I wasn't far from it.

Emotionally, the insanity of Jamie's addiction affected the entire family. I would descend into screaming rages at the slightest provocation. I was in deep denial regarding how much his life choices were affecting me.

As a woman and a mother navigating life, I experience great joy when my loved ones are thriving and happy. However, when they suffer, it impacts me deeply at the core of my being. It transforms me into a fierce warrior, ready to defend or sacrifice myself to protect my children. Yet, it has been said to me and is written in many sacred scriptures that your children come through you but possess their own souls and destinies. They are of God, the Creator, from the mother/father God, and it is to the Creator that they will return. Simply put, I'm just a custodian of my children, meant to love and guide them as best I can. I don't own them. That axiom was presented to me to once again confront the truth of being a mother. I understood the message, but it overwhelmed me, and I felt completely powerless to stop my pain.

In the meantime, Amaya had moved to Santa Fe, so she called to check in on me and provide her new address and phone number. I was ecstatic to hear about her relocation.

As always, Amaya got right to the point. "Wendy, I hear a great sadness in your voice. What's going on? Is it Jamie?"

I explained to her the nightmare of his journey up to that moment.

"All right, then," she said. "Let's get you in here for some work."

Over the years, I have been challenged to the core by my work with Amaya and the spirits she channels; however, I sought out the healing they offered and embraced it with deep gratitude. After several bodywork sessions, Amaya said, "Wendy, I can't help you anymore. You need to start going to Al-Anon meetings. I want you to attend three meetings a week for a while. Then, we'll see what happens."

I was aware of Al-Anon, and it had been suggested to me as a tool for our family by one of Jamie's rehabilitation centers. Al-Anon is called a "fellowship of relatives and friends of alcoholics who share their experience, strength, and hope, in order to solve their common problems." The organization says, "We believe alcoholism is a family illness and that changed attitudes can aid recovery." Of course, they include drug addiction.

I felt ashamed to step into meetings until Amaya was so adamant about it. I trusted her implicitly. All my years of spiritual work, meditation, and healing began to quietly come together when I joined the circle at the start of Al-Anon meetings. As I sat and listened to the twelve steps, traditions, and the different shares in my first meeting, I could hardly breathe as the acute pain I was feeling surfaced. Al-Anon became a safe and appropriate place for me to heal. I could express whatever I felt without judgment from anyone in the meeting. Everyone understood. There was no cross talk during sharing, and there was no right or wrong way to work the program. Every process was a suggestion, so I could take what I needed and leave the rest. This was a fail-safe program for my overachieving, have-to-do-everything-right personality.

It took several meetings before I got up the nerve to share. When I did, my voice was small, weak, and full of fear and anxiety. It didn't even sound like my voice, but no one cared. They just listened and occasionally nodded their heads. For me, the progressive healing that occurred through attending meetings and working the twelve steps was profoundly deep. The group of strangers was from every walk of life and diverse religious and political backgrounds, but all of them were developing a miraculous relationship with the God of their understanding.

I learned about letting go and letting God and slowly delved deep into myself to feel and heal the damage from growing up with my mother's alcoholism. It was as if I were cleaning out the hard drive of my psyche, discovering operating systems I didn't even know I had that were influencing my every thought and attitude. I began to understand that I was powerless over the disease. Using the program's tools to recognize and release old patterns, I started to build a new normal. I was coming around to a paradigm shift in my consciousness—turning over the care of my beloved, drug-addicted son to the God of *my* understanding. Suddenly, my relationship with God became very, very personal.

It seemed that the more I grew spiritually, the more I had to confront fear and my own dysfunction. I realize this seems reasonable, as issues come to the surface to be healed, but that knowledge doesn't make it any less challenging. If I practice the three A's of Awareness, Acceptance, and Action, I can gradually work through my seemingly endless character defects and life issues with faith, love, and humor.

In 2005, we had another opportunity to move—this time to Santa Barbara. We had spent the last three summers there so that Tucker could enroll in a tutorial program to help him with his dyslexia. We felt we had more educational options there than in Santa Fe, and we loved living by the sea.

Santa Barbara is as spectacularly beautiful as Santa Fe. We have a mountain range behind us and the Pacific Ocean lapping at the shoreline in front. On a clear day, we can gaze out toward a string of islands across the channel.

Within months of moving to the area, I found an Al-Anon meeting I liked, allowing me to continue with my own recovery. I had come to terms with the extent of the damage that my mother's alcoholic behavior, my string of failed boyfriends, an unsuccessful marriage, and my eldest son's ongoing struggles with drug addiction had caused both to my psyche and my physical body.

One day in 2018, news came to me that Jamie had relapsed yet again. At this point, he had been suffering from the disease of addiction on and off for about twenty years. When I receive news like this, especially after a short sober period, it feels like a massive gut punch. It completely shatters me. Each time he chose sobriety, I couldn't help but think, *Maybe this is it—it will stick.*

I sat down on the window seat in our bedroom, took a breath, and said the Serenity Prayer I had learned in Al-Anon. I could feel my benevolent teachers in spirit gather around me.

"Well," I said out loud, "I know this disease will kill him at some point if he stays in the addiction."

What I also *knew* was that, should this drug addiction cause his death, he would be completely taken care of. His team of angelic guides would be right there to guide him to the healing his soul would need, and he would not suffer from this horrible disease any longer in his physical body.

In a word, he would be completely fine. On the other hand, I would be completely shattered, devastated, in pain, and struck by grief down to my very core.

"So, dear one," my guides chimed in, "what is the real issue for you here, then?"

I sat quietly with this for a little while before I answered.

"The *real* issue for me? I am terrified of the pain of losing a child; I don't know if I can bear it."

And there it was.

All my enabling over the years was driven by my pain and fear of personally suffering his death. In truth, it had nothing to do with him.

I sat for a while longer, trying to take this in.

"Okay, God," I said out loud, "here is the deal: I am going to show up. I know it is going to hurt like hell, but I am not pushing these emotions away anymore, now that I understand.

I see how this has been affecting myself and my family, and it is within my power to change myself."

I know my son is in good hands; he always has been.

It was my fear of the discomfort, fear, and pain I would feel that had kept me from "letting go and letting God."

CHAPTER 12

Pick Up the Hoof

"It's not about the horse."

—WYATT WEBB

Years ago, Wyatt Webb, the founder of the Equine Experience at Miraval Spa in Tucson, Arizona, wrote a beautiful book called *It's Not About the Horse*. In it, he shared his personal journey regarding his life and recovery from addiction.

When I had the opportunity to participate in one of his Equine Experiences in Tucson, I was thrilled, yet a bit nervous. Wyatt was a large man who resembled a crusty old cowboy. He had a strong presence that was expressed through his quiet demeanor. I sensed he was a no-nonsense therapist as he led his group equine therapy sessions—and I was absolutely right in that assumption.

He guided our group through an hour or so of instruction, leading each one of us through particular exercises while the rest of the group sat in observation on benches alongside the ring. Our therapy horse appeared somewhat bedraggled—my guess was that she had been rescued from a kill pen. However, she was very healthy.

Wyatt's questions were direct and penetrating as he addressed us individually. I realized that I was being exposed; layers being peeled away in a group setting can be very uncomfortable. However, having many years of experience working with my spirit teachers, I knew well to trust the process. Even though I had never done something like this in a group setting, Wyatt's strength and skill as a therapist were very evident to me, so I tried to let go as best I could.

When it was time to work with the horse, Wyatt explained that we were to approach her, pick up her hoof, and clean out debris from the bottom of the hoof with a special pick he had given us to use. We could choose to do either the front or the back. If she did not raise her hoof for us, we were not to lean on her shoulder to push her off balance to do this, as I had done for years when I was riding.

When it was my turn, I was third in line with maybe thirteen people ahead of me. I walked into the ring and stood next to Wyatt. He looked at me and handed me my pick. I slowly walked over to the horse, turned my left shoulder toward her left shoulder, ran my hand down the inside of her leg, squared my stance to pick up her hoof. Nothing . . . I tried again; she wouldn't move.

"Squeeze the muscle behind her hoof," Wyatt chimed in.

Nothing . . . She would not budge.

"Harder!" Wyatt said. "You won't hurt her."

I squeezed harder, but once again, she didn't budge.

"Try again. Be intentional; ask her," Wyatt said.

Nothing; I tried the back leg, but I couldn't get this horse to "pick up her hoof."

I stood up, looked at Wyatt, and he motioned for me to come and stand next to him (he was sitting on a stool). He then called the next person up, and so it continued through the group.

At that moment, I was not self-conscious about standing in front of the class at all, as I was completely baffled about what issue within me was preventing her from lifting her hoof. I knew, however, that if I could calm myself down, I would understand the lesson.

Now, I was the last person standing next to Wyatt, and suddenly, I felt this tremendous energy flowing from the horse directly into my heart.

"You don't believe I am going to pick up my hoof." Her words lit up my whole being; never had I experienced anything like this. The love with which she shared this truth made my eyes well up.

I turned to look at Wyatt, stammering, "I know what it is— she told me." He looked deep into my eyes, smiled, and handed me the pick.

As I approached her, she raised her hoof even before I touched her.

Later that evening, while I was at the bar in the restaurant, a group of about five women approached me. I recognized them as part of the group I had been with earlier in the day with Wyatt. They surrounded me with exclamations of empathy!

"Oh my God, you had to stand up there next to Wyatt—we all felt terrible for you. But you handled it with so much grace and presence; it was amazing to watch you go through that." There was a lot of light bouncing around our conversation. It had never occurred to me that those women were having that experience. I got a chance to share my experience with them, and I was grateful for that.

I came to realize that my healing experience not only affected me but also the people around me.

At times, when I am struggling with something, the first thing I write in my journal is, *PICK UP THE HOOF*, so I can check in with myself. Even setting an intention and moving toward a goal won't work for me if deep inside I don't believe it will succeed.

Epilogue

One day, my son Tucker—a nineteen-year-old deep thinker—was struggling with the state of the world, our planet, our government, and war. These sentiments felt very familiar to me. As a young man and an undergraduate pursuing a degree in philosophy at university, he loved to provoke me into philosophical discussions or, on most occasions, arguments. He also challenged my lifelong passion for mysticism, which he considered to be very unscientific and a bunch of "hooey falooey."

On this particular day, he stood in our kitchen, filled with anger and frustration. These moments could really test my patience, and that day he was bent on provoking me. Tall and thin, towering over me with his hands on his hips and fire in his eyes, he said, "Well, Mom . . . what have you done with your life that is so great?"

He was going for broke.

I knew that when he looked at me, he saw a middle-aged woman who lived in a lovely house and had mostly been a stay-at-home mom. To him, I was living a life of leisure, free from the worries of finishing university, starting a career, or figuring out where I would live. I didn't have to stress about making enough money to pay the bills. In his mind, how could I possibly understand the life issues he was grappling with?

I took in a breath, thinking of the extensive volunteer community work I do. I almost took the bait, but instead, in a nanosecond, I sent up a silent prayer. "Help . . . words." I took a deep breath, stood up tall, and felt the power of the mother energy drop in. I looked him straight in the eye and said in a very strong voice, "I am *looking at it*!"

He was completely speechless. A look of innocence and surprise flashed across his beautiful brown eyes, and my heart melted.

He didn't see it coming.

My older son, Jamie, has been clean and sober for seven years. He returned to college and earned his certification as a drug and alcohol counselor. The certification process is extremely rigorous. He is deeply involved in the recovery community and works full-time in this field.

Addiction is an insidious disease that requires a great deal of humility, gratitude, and respect. Seven years ago, he made the decision that he was ready to do the work of climbing out of a dark hellhole, and thankfully, the recovery community is a strong and powerful ally. As someone told me many years ago, "Wendy, Jamie has a higher power, and you are not it!" He has fully embraced that higher power, and it has been transformational.

Looking back at the two events that informed the beginning of this book, I finally realize why I was suddenly cursing at God, Jesus, Mary, and Joseph. I realized that this sudden awareness was no accident. The second was deciding to put the story about "the Hill" at the beginning.

I knew that I wasn't just angry with God and Jesus, but that I *resented* them. When I looked up the meaning of the word, the dictionary defined it as, "A feeling of indignant displeasure or persistent ill will at something regarded as wrong, insulting or injury."

This resentment created what my teachers, channeled by Amaya, would say to me: "You grieve the loss of self, dear one." I never fully understood what that meant, honestly. But I have a clearer understanding of it today. The energy of the resentment I felt toward God, although buried deep in my psyche, kept me vibrationally out of alignment with Source energy (God). I am one with God; every fiber of my being is created from Source energy. When I lose this connection, when I forget who I am, then I feel the grief of loss of self.

When I quietly absorbed this new word, substituting "anger" with "resentment" felt jarring. It was dark and almost menacing, leaving me feeling very uncomfortable and deeply guilty. God, the Creator—Source energy, vibrating at a pure frequency of love—resides in all things. It is in the beauty of our planet, the magnificence of Creation, and the stunning moments of humanity. There is also darkness, destruction, and the witnessing of the horrific actions humans can inflict on one another, which is nearly unfathomable and terrifying.

But then I come back to this quote by Ceanne DeRohan: "Do you choose love or fear? Unconditional love would choose both by bringing our fears within love and finding out what they have to offer."

The darkness *and* the light.

This feeling of resentment has dwelled deep within me, buried for eons. It was not until I was willing to become uncomfortable enough to finally understand these repressed emotions, and work through them with humility and trust, that I could release them. The deep gratitude I experienced while working on this book, along with the personal growth and guidance I received from the higher realms, was astounding. I learned to lean into the feeling of being uncomfortable in my emotional body and listen for the gift.

This is the gift of being uncomfortable.

Take a breath. Life is sacred.